Linda Lawrence Hunt

BOLD SPIRIT

Linda Lawrence Hunt, a former associate professor of English at Whitworth College, now directs The Krista Foundation for Global Citizenship. An engaging speaker and award-winning freelance writer, Hunt traveled across America and to Norway to reconstruct the silenced story of Helga Estby's epic journey. *Bold Spirit* won the 2004 Willa Cather Literary Award for nonfiction, the Washington State Book Award, and the Pacific Northwest Booksellers Award. She lives in Spokane, Washington, with her husband Jim.

www.boldspiritacrossamerica.com

BOLD SPIRIT

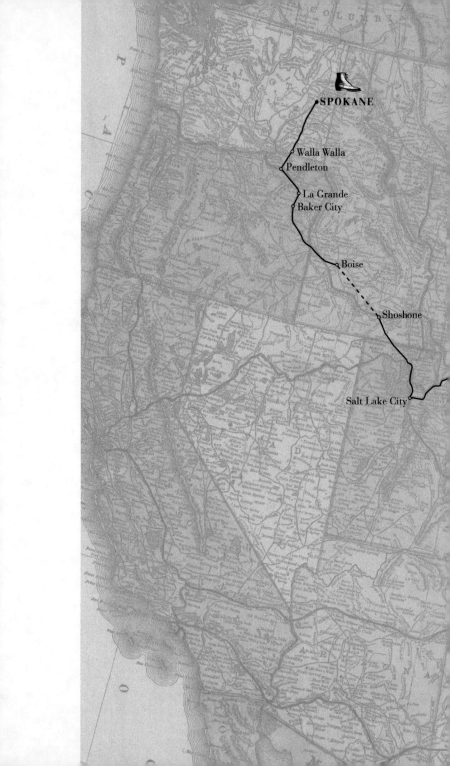

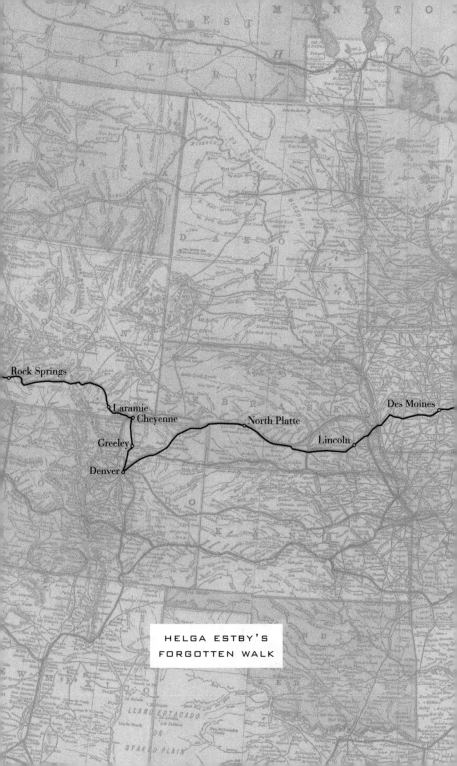

Rock Springs

Laramie
Cheyenne

Greeley

Denver

North Platte

Lincoln

Des Moines

HELGA ESTBY'S
FORGOTTEN WALK

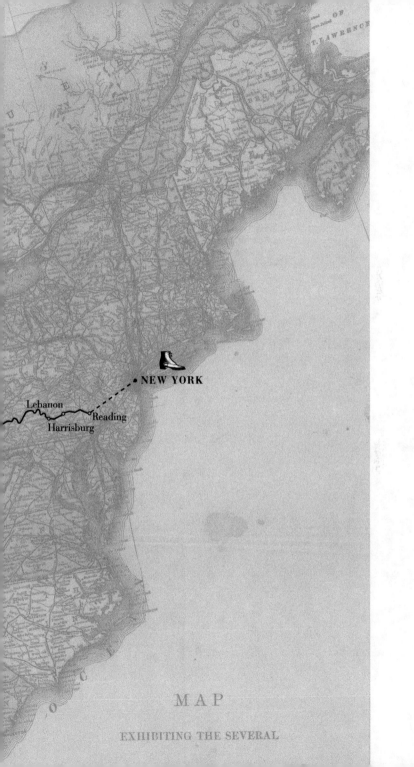

Lebanon

Harrisburg Reading

● NEW YORK

BOLD SPIRIT

HELGA ESTBY'S FORGOTTEN WALK
ACROSS VICTORIAN AMERICA

Linda Lawrence Hunt

FOREWORD BY SUE ARMITAGE

C. S. Ricker,   1311 Wash. Ave. S. Minneapolis.

ANCHOR BOOKS
A DIVISION OF RANDOM HOUSE, INC.
NEW YORK

FIRST ANCHOR BOOKS EDITION, JANUARY 2005

Copyright © 2003 by Linda Lawrence Hunt

Anchor Books and colophon are registered trademarks of
Random House, Inc.

Map Courtesy of the Library of Congress

Library of Congress Cataloging-in-Publication Data
Hunt, Linda, 1940–
Bold spirit : Helga Estby's forgotten walk across Victorian America / Linda
Lawrence Hunt ; foreword by Sue Armitage.
p. cm.
Includes bibliographical references and index.
ISBN 1-4000-7993-4
1. United States—Description and travel.   2. United States—Social life
and customs—1865–1918.   3. Estby, Helga, b. 1860—Travel—United
States.   4. Estby, Clara, b. 1876—Travel—United States.   5. Walking—
United States—History—19th century.   6. Norwegian Americans—
Biography.   7. Mothers and daughters—United States—Biography.
E168.H94   2005
973.8'7'0922—dc22
[B] 2004057372

Author photograph © Jim Hunt

www.anchorbooks.com

Printed in the United States of America
10   9   8

To

Thelma Portch

and

Dorothy, Daryll, Darillyn, and Doug Bahr,

who became keepers of this family story

and to

Evelyn Christensen

another ordinary woman who

lives an extraordinary life

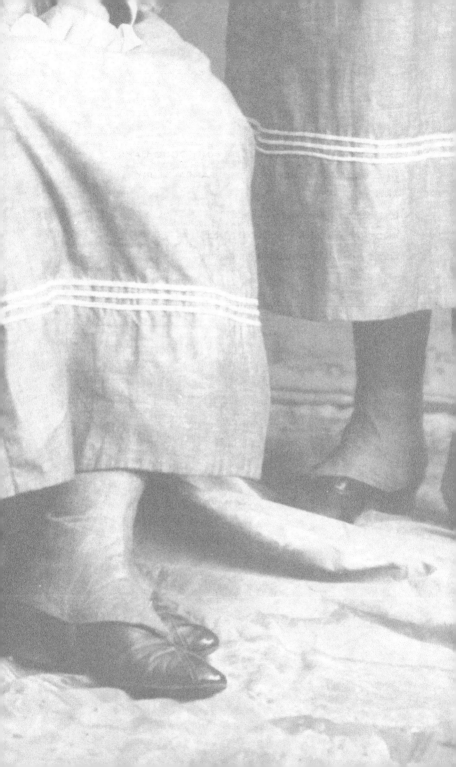

Contents

Foreword

The amazing story of Helga Estby's walk across America, which you will read in the following pages, was almost lost from history. Even now, after all of Linda Hunt's diligent research and imaginative retelling, there are aspects of Helga's story that remain mysterious. Although some readers may be frustrated by these lingering mysteries, I suggest that they give us opportunities to think about what we call "history." The historical record tells us about how people acted in the past, but it often does not tell us why. It is the job of professional historians to provide plausible reasons for the actions of the past. But the truth is that even the most famous and well-documented historical personages contain pockets of mystery and take actions that we do not fully understand. If this is true for the great and famous, think how much more likely it is to be true for an immigrant woman like Helga Estby. Think also about how many life stories of ordinary people have been lost to history because there are no surviving records. The truly amazing thing about Helga Estby is that she did something extraordinary, and her story still remained unknown—until now. Her erasure should prompt us all to think about how little of the past we really know and encourage us to think about how to preserve more of our present-day lives and concerns (tomorrow's historical record).

Every day we make decisions about which events are important and which are not. In fact, our historical record begins right now in the present with this daily process of inclusion and omission. In her conclusion to Helga Estby's story, Linda Hunt invites us to think about the different kinds of omission she calls silencing. In that contemplation are some hard lessons that bear directly on our sense of history. Several lessons occur to me; doubtless each of you can add to the list. First, we expect the already great and famous to do great things, but we easily overlook the achievements of the more humble among us. Second, we prefer predictable stories with easily understood motivations; unexpected actions undertaken for uncertain reasons make us uncomfortable. Third, people who act too far from their expected norms are embarrassments to those around them. How much truer is this likely to be when the historical actor is poor and female?

Throughout history, silencing has been the fate of most women. Thanks to Linda Hunt's interest and extraordinary persistence, Helga Estby has escaped that common fate. Finally then, this is not just Helga Estby's story but Linda Hunt's as well, for in the following pages she shows us just how much silenced history can be recovered when we really want to know.

—*Sue Armitage*, Washington State University

Preface

It was late one evening in 1984 when I read eighth-grader Doug Bahr's seven-page essay entered in the Washington State History Day Contest. This farm son from Wilbur, through the encouragement of his mother, Dorothy, and older sister, Darillyn, told a stunning story in "Grandma Walks from Coast to Coast." This brief family story of a mother and daughter's walk captivated my imagination and curiosity. Who was this Norwegian immigrant, Helga Estby? Whatever gave Helga and her daughter Clara the courage to attempt such a journey? I recently had read Peter Jenkin's observations and experiences on his contemporary cross-continent trek in *A Walk Across America*, a story that attracted immense national interest. I felt certain a mother and daughter's observations and experiences across an unsettled continent almost one hundred years earlier would prove compelling. Was there more to the story?

In subsequent investigation, I found that little was known about Helga's audacious gamble to earn the $10,000 wager offered by unknown sponsors for completion of the journey. Behind on paying taxes and the mortgage, she was desperate to save the 160-acre Mica Creek farm and home built by her husband, Ole, for their family of nine children. Hers was a woman's story, and like most ordinary mothers of her era, her active participation in life was not valued as part of America's historical record. Even more telling, Helga's choice to leave home, and the subsequent tragedy of loss, led to such anger in the family that they did not value her remarkable story either. Her walk across the United States with her daughter Clara remained a silenced topic within the family for over seventy years.

Because of this lack of recognition, the most difficult aspect of rediscovering Helga Estby's life is the paucity of primary resources. For example, no diaries, letters, or art sketches remain from Helga and Clara's trip, although Helga wrote many letters and kept a diary. Nor do the hundreds of manuscript pages she wrote still exist. Her children are all dead. Furthermore, the children's lifelong condemnation of their mother's actions led to fateful choices about her memoirs. It was unfathomable to them that Helga's writings might contribute significantly to a fuller picture of American history. Like the history of most women at the end of the nineteenth century, her life story became silenced partially by what I call "negation through neglect." But it was silenced also by intention.

A short poem from a Scottish psychologist, R.D. Laing, in *Vital Lies, Simple Truths*, addresses this neglect and the failure to recognize the importance of family stories of *all* people, not just the culturally privileged. It speaks also to the truth that, until recently, academia ignored the history of most women in the American story. The poem states:

The range of what we think and do
is limited by what we fail to notice
And because we fail to notice
that we fail to notice
there is little we can do
to change
until we notice
how failing to notice
shapes our thoughts and deeds

Because Helga's immediate family "failed to notice" the importance of her endeavor, they did not keep any letters from the trip, or pass her stories orally through the family. Even more distressing, they destroyed the hundreds of pages of her first-person account. The necessity for creative historical detective work to unearth her life inaugurated years of research.

I call this approach to the reconstruction of Helga Estby's life a "rag-rug history." In Scandinavia, resourceful women historically collected the discards and remnants of previously used fabrics from all possible sources. From these worn castoffs, often considered of little value to others, they wove together a weft of rags to create incredibly strong and durable artistic rugs. In contrast, early American women usually made quilts from good-quality remnants intentionally saved and treasured. Frugal immigrants continued to create rag rugs to warm their pioneer homes. Contemporary rag-rug weavers still go on hunting expeditions to search for the fabrics from ordinary lives, such as torn and tattered chenille bedspreads, blue jeans, corduroy, and calico. Often weavers will alert their friends and family to help discover old fabrics that others rarely find useful. From these they collect the textures and colors that provide the beauty and interest for today's creations. The weaver takes these piles of ripped rags, packs the strips tightly together to prevent unraveling, and then, using a beater bar on a loom with warping thread, creates a durable, useful family rug.

My search to find as many remnants of her story as possible led to my own trips across America, and to Norway to learn about Helga's childhood. Scraps of information gathered from our nation's rich resources in local historical societies, community and university libraries, and museums became the fabrics of her story. The strong golden thread that wove the rag-rug remnants together came from newspaper accounts of Helga's visits with reporters along the railroad routes. These eyewitness accounts verified her itinerary and provided a general timetable. More important, they offered a rich vein of stories, although admittedly, they were limited by what a reporter asked and by what Helga and Clara chose to report. Little existed in these accounts of the ordinary daily challenges the women faced in meeting basic survival needs, such as finding food, water, and shelter during the long distances between towns in the West. Nor do reporters show how they coped with the life-threatening extremes of cold and heat, sore muscles and feet, women's hygiene, electric storms, or dangerous wildlife. Nor do we read of the many specific human kindnesses they say eased the journey, or of the ways nature sometimes refreshed their spirits. However, the varied tone and observations within the reporter's accounts did provide insights into the attitudes the writers held about the two women "globetrotters." The tenor of a newspaper, whether primarily interested in international and national issues or local and human-interest stories, affected the coverage. Whether scant or lengthy articles, newspaper errors sometimes emerged. It is also impossible to know if Helga or Clara embellished their adventures. The consistencies of their accounts throughout the newspaper coverage, however, suggest genuine experiences. If anything, their reporting of the travails seem understated.

Whenever people heard portions of Helga's bold trek, they worked eagerly to help me find additional rag remnants of this nearly discarded life story. The generous gifts of memory and artifacts from the remaining Estby family, a family that does "notice" the importance of Helga's achievement, augmented these institutional resources.

During this research I discovered a refreshing image that symbolizes the new scholarship emerging on previously neglected women. When Norwegian artist Aasta Hansteen came to America, she was enchanted with the sunflower image that some early

American feminists used as a symbol of a woman's claim to light, and air, and an optimistic spirit. She introduced this symbol on her return to Norway, and the Norwegian Feminist Society adopted it as their official symbol right about the time of Helga's walk. Helga's courageous story, once shrouded in silence, now can be linked with other women's stories emerging in a new American history, a history open to giving light and air to the many voices in our land. My hope is that *Bold Spirit* contributes an enduring remnant that reflects the irrepressible spirit, intelligence, and abundant love for family and America that Helga Estby's adventurous life illuminates.

—Linda Lawrence Hunt

BOLD SPIRIT

Eight-year-old Thelma Estby, bewildered by the sudden death of her father from meningitis, moved to her Grandma Helga Estby's home in Spokane, Washington, in 1924. Living with her beloved grandma was the one comfort in her new life as she adjusted to a strange school and unfamiliar neighborhood. The child sensed that her grandma understood how much she missed her dad. Sometimes Thelma and her grandma Helga rocked on the porch swing that her grandpa Ole built. Then, grandma told stories of what Thelma's father, Arthur, was like as a young boy living on the Estby's farm at Mica Creek, southeast of Spokane, Washington. Thelma loved hearing these stories, their lively memories easing the empty loss she felt. But more often the grandmother and grandchild sat in companionable silence as little Thelma grieved the loss of her dad, and Helga grieved the death of her fifth son. They found warmth and joy in each other, drawn together to relieve the sorrow surrounding them both. Even the scent of her grandmother's Azure of Roses perfume comforted her.[1]

Thelma thrived on the special attention her grandmother gave her. Even at sixty-four years, with a crippled knee, Helga Estby loved to be on the go. When her small widow's pension arrived each month from Ole's trade union death benefit, Helga took Thelma on a trolley ride over the Spokane River to downtown. Often they watched Spokane Falls tumble over the basalt rocks, enchanted with its beauty and power, and then paused at the water's edge to feed scraps of stale bread to the ducks. Usually they stopped at the stately Crescent department store where Helga found colorful fabrics, threads, ribbons, and buttons to make special clothes for Thelma and her dolls. Sometimes they strolled uptown past the twin towers of Our Lady of Lourdes Cathedral, which Ole helped build, and continued down through the stately tree-lined streets of Browne's Addition. Here the turn-of-the-century mansions and formal gardens spoke of a world of wealth unfamiliar to the farm child more at home with wheat fields and sunflowers. To Thelma's surprise, many fashionably dressed women in this prestigious neighborhood seemed to know her grandmother and spoke to her with respect. They were obviously interested in Helga's thoughts and friendship, something Thelma also noticed among Norwegian-American women in their own middle-class neighborhood on Mallon Street.[2] On summer days, they joined

---

Thelma Estby, mid-1920s, Spokane, Washington.

Courtesy Portch/Bahr Family Photograph Collection.
Detail of this photograph on page xxiv.

the throngs of people riding the carousel at Natatorium Park or rode the train east to Lake Coeur d'Alene where Helga visited a friend from her earlier work in the women's suffrage movement.

If daytime gave Thelma fun adventures with her grandma, nighttime gave her an abiding sense of security in her grandma Helga's faith. Helga loved to read, and Thelma liked climbing under the quilt in her grandma's pine bed while grandma read to her from one of her favorite books, *The Lamplighter*, over and over. Second only in popularity to *Uncle Tom's Cabin*, this popular religious novel showed how suffering, self-discipline, and devotion can form a person's character in positive ways. The main character, Gerty, was also an unhappy eight-year-old girl who had lost her parents. Neglected and abused, she developed into a troublesome orphan with an explosive temper. Eventually, a loving blind woman adopted Gerty and taught two truths to the little girl. First, that "The world is full of trials, everyone gets a share," and second, "Even in the midst of our distress, we can look to God in faith and love." Thelma loved the reassurance of hearing how the sad, fatherless child grew into a strong, happy woman.[3]

Helga told Thelma how she also suddenly lost her own father when she was just two years old, so she seemed to understand her granddaughter's loss. Born in Christiana (now Oslo), Norway, on May 30 in 1860, Helga knew her parents enjoyed a union of genuine love because she saw how this unexpected loss left her mother grief stricken for years.[4] But she told Thelma that good experiences still came after their family's distress, especially when her mother remarried a merchant when Helga was seven years old. Because her stepfather, Mr. Haug, had money, the family sent Helga to a private school in Norway that included instruction in English, science, and religion.[5] Coming to America when she was eleven was another wonderful surprise in Helga's life that happened because of her mother's remarriage.

Every evening, even if their meal seemed quite simple, Helga set the table with white linen, china dishes, silver napkin rings, and whatever flowers were blooming in their garden. The family loved music, often listening to classical musical on the radio. Although they could not afford a piano, Aunt Ida played the harmonica, Uncle Bill enjoyed the violin, and grandma loved to sing, even if off-key. For their festive Norwegian Christmas Eve celebration, Helga always made lefse, sour-creme pudding with almonds and lingonberries, and homemade wine from the backyard cherry tree.[6]

Although much in her grandmother's home gave Thelma comfort and pleasure, she sensed something was not quite right in the family. To the young child, it felt as though a cloud hovered over her grandmother inside the house. Whenever Helga wanted to talk politics, Thelma noticed that the family either ignored her or just cut her off rudely. It upset Thelma when her aunts or uncles said mean things to their mother. This seemed to happen most if Helga wanted to talk about women's rights and the recent suffrage laws allowing women to vote, something that Helga's daughters resolutely refused to do.[7] She wondered why her grandma never talked back, seeming instead to slip into a silent, unreachable world of her own. Thelma noticed that when this happened, Grandma Helga's face became melancholy. Was this why she rarely laughed? She seemed to be treated so differently outside their home. Yet, Thelma never heard her grandma say anything judgmental about her family or other people.

She also wondered if this was why her grandma often retreated upstairs where she created in a room of her own. In this upper room, Helga painted with oils, pastels, and watercolors and worked on writing a book. Helga considered this her private space, so Thelma felt quite special when Grandma invited her up. One morning, when the Indian-summer sun was pouring through the north window, she saw that her grandma was leafing through hundreds of pages of yellow foolscap paper. When Helga saw Thelma, she hugged the child into the folds of her long Victorian skirt and said, "Honey, be sure to take care of this story for me." But Thelma had no idea what "story" she was talking about.[8]

Forty-five years elapsed before Thelma discovered just what she had been asked to treasure. She was appalled to learn that this story had been so silenced by the entire family that it was almost lost forever. Nor had her grandma, who loved to read adventure stories to her at bedtime, ever breathed a word of her own grand adventure. When Thelma learned the truth, she vowed to fulfill her grandmother's request and became the story keeper, passing the legacy of Helga's courageous spirit to her own children and grandchildren. *Bold Spirit* emerged because Thelma believed in the power and value of preserving her family stories.

1
ON FOOT TO NEW YORK

*Should they survive the trip their reminiscences will
undoubtedly attract great attention.*

—DAILY CHRONICLE
SPOKANE, WASHINGTON, MAY 4, 1896

Helga Estby, a thirty-six-year-old Norwegian immigrant, woke early on a mid-June morning in 1896 and slipped on her full-length gray Victorian skirt, simple wool jacket, and new leather shoes. She was eager to leave Boise, Idaho, before 6 A.M. to avoid walking during the scorching midday sun in southern Idaho, a hazard she had failed to consider earlier. Her daughter Clara, an artistic, intelligent, and pretty eighteen year old, helped fill their small satchels with emergency necessities: a Smith-and-Wesson revolver and a red-pepper spray gun to thwart dangerous highwaymen or wild animals, a compass and map, a few medical supplies, a lantern for night walking, photographs of themselves to sell, and a curling iron for Clara's soft hair.[1]

Even when carrying a little food, their bundles weighed less than eight pounds. Wanting to travel light, neither brought a change of clothes, but Helga packed a notebook and pen to record their experiences, and Clara brought materials for sketching.[2] Perhaps more important, they carried a document from Mayor Belt of their hometown of Spokane, Washington, that introduced Helga as "a lady of good character and reputation" and commending her and her daughter to "the kindly consideration of all persons with whom they may have contact."[3] As vital as a calling card to open doors, this introduction was especially useful with people in politics and the media.

They left Boise grateful for the kind considerations shown to them in Idaho's new capital city. The *Idaho Daily Statesman* had alerted readers of the mother and daughter's arrival and of their brave quest across America. Unlike a small Washington town whose residents refused to let them buy food or find shelter because people suspected the women were "undeserving vagrants," Boise residents showed respect for their "positive spirits and physical energy." They offered the women opportunities to clean and cook and bought their photographs to restore their depleted funds.[4]

For thirty days, the unaccompanied women had successfully traversed by foot more than 450 miles during the wettest spring in thirty-three years. Having left Spokane on May 5, they followed the rail route south through Washington and Oregon, then trudged east through the spring snows and thaws over the Blue Mountain range, and on through the swollen river waters threatening the Boise valley.

There had been only three days without rain since they started, and they arrived in Boise on June 5 with the city in alarm as the raging Boise River reached flood stage. Their journey astonished people, especially that "the women did not seem discouraged."[5]

In truth, it was deep discouragement and near despair that set Helga on this dangerous path to solve her family's desperate financial plight. Since the devastating economic depression of 1893, and her husband's accidents, they simply could not pay the mortgage or taxes on their home and farmland near Spokane. Foreclosure loomed during the spring of 1896, sending Helga into a state of fear compounded by sorrow as she also grieved the loss of her beloved twelve-year-old son, Henry, who had died in January.[6]

When she learned of a $10,000 wager offered by "eastern parties" connected to the fashion industry to a woman who would walk across America, Helga decided to try.[7] She could not bear seeing her eight remaining children become homeless and thrown into destitution. She explained to her family and friends, who considered her decision outrageous, that she simply had "to make a stake some way," for she did not want to lose the farm. This was the only way she could see to save it. Most of her neighbors in the Norwegian enclave of farms in Mica Creek considered her choice both impossible and immoral, "not something women do."[8]

The sponsors wanted to prove the physical endurance of women, at a time when many still considered it fashionable to be dependent and weak. Helga accepted certain stipulations within the contract, even agreeing to wear the "reform costume," a bicycle skirt that sponsors wanted her to advertise once she got to Salt Lake City. She and Clara were allowed to leave with only $5 a piece and then had to earn their way across; were to visit the state capitals in the west; and were to get the signatures of important political persons along the way.[9] When she visited Idaho's Governor William J. McConnell at the State House, a friend of Mayor Belt's, his expression of interest in their walk and his personal note on their introductory document increased her awareness of the importance of their attempt.[10]

As she left Boise with her resolve fortified, and their supplies replenished, Helga began to worry about meeting another stipulation of the contract: The deadline for their walk required they be in New York City within seven months. The rains slowed their earlier days, and it took several days of working in Boise to earn enough money to continue. They needed to arrive in early December, but the sponsors did allow additional days if they became ill.[11] Because getting lost in America's vast continent in the west was one of the

Helga and Clara planned to follow the railroad routes to avoid getting lost and to find places with food and shelter.

Courtesy Library of Congress. LC Railroad Maps, 64; digital Id g3701p rr000640.
Detail of this photograph on page 8.

1890

Matthews, Northrup & Co's

Official Railroad Map

OF THE

UNITED STATES,
DOMINION OF CANADA
AND MEXICO

PERFECTED TO DATE FROM LATEST AUTHENTIC SOURCES.

ENGRAVED AND PRINTED BY

Matthews, Northrup & Co.

Buffalo, & New York.

dangers, Helga and Clara had planned to follow the railway routes, including the Union Pacific to Denver.

Although enduring drenching rains and wading through hip-deep flood waters in Idaho failed to sap Helga's spirits, it did make her receptive to advice on short cuts. Outside of Shoshone they apparently decided to leave the rails, probably hoping to find a shortcut route that had been used by pioneers seeking a faster way from Pocatello to Boise during the Oregon Trail and gold rush days. For three days Helga and Clara wandered "without a mouthful to eat," eventually becoming lost in the Snake River lava beds of southern Idaho, a treacherous maze of cracked lava, crevices, and sagebrush.[12] Jagged rocks tore up their thin leather shoes and temperatures in the mid-eighties smothered them in their long Victorian dresses. Even more troubling, the fear of rattlesnakes hovered around every step in this barren moonscape land.

During these days of gnawing hunger, intense heat, and disorientation, when all the vocal criticism of the folly of their venture looked frighteningly true, Helga may have faced her own fears over the real and present dangers of this odyssey. Her Scandinavian neighbors saw her as a "determined" woman who achieves what "she makes up her mind" to do, and Helga's actions often reflected her inner confidence and quiet faith.[13] She had struggled earlier with anxieties, especially during pivotal challenges, such as the time of a debilitating accident or during prairie fires and tornadoes on the Minnesota prairie. Her belief since childhood in the power of God undoubtedly led her to pray for Divine help as she and Clara grew weaker, seemingly helpless in their own ability to decipher how to get out of this strange land.

But the stark danger of their present situation could have caused her to wonder if she naively underestimated the risks she placed Clara and herself in, and too blithely dismissed the fears of those who counseled her to stay home with her husband, Ole, and their children. This life-threatening detour was a mistake so costly that Clara and she risked leaving their bleached bones on the lava beds as the sole surviving remnant of their courageous venture. Helga knew, because they no longer were near the rails, that if they died her husband and children might never know what happened to them, a fear she had not considered with all the other warnings. As the moon rose over the eerie land on their third night lost among the lava rocks, Helga pondered and prayed. Her hope and faith intermingled with alarm at a seemingly impossible situation that her resourcefulness might not be able to solve.

2 MOTHERHOOD ON A MINNESOTA PRAIRIE

*They were very poor and desperately needed
money living in a one-room sod shanty.
It must have been very hard for Helga
after living well in her childhood.*

—THELMA PORTCH, GRANDDAUGHTER

*We lived out on the prairie.
We never mingled with anybody.*

—IDA ESTBY, DAUGHTER

Helga's walk across America was not her first
major journey undertaken to create a better life. At
eleven years old, Helga traveled from Norway with
her mother, Karen, on the ship *Oder* and arrived in
Manistee, Michigan, on August 12, 1871. Her stepfather had gone ahead to America to start life anew and
had settled in this lake town, a thriving economic
center for the Scandinavians working nearby in the
twenty-four lumber mills.[1] Although a devastating
fire destroyed the prosperous town that same year, by
1873 two hundred new buildings reflected the expec-
tation and determination of the optimistic popula-

17

tion. Helga attended schools in America for enough time to become proficient in written and oral English, and she loved her new country. A bright child, she found great pleasure in reading. As an only child, she enjoyed how her bilingual ability helped her Norwegian mother and father negotiate in their new land.

During the 1870s, with a growing population of nearly 10,000 residents, Manistee was embroiled in raging debates over the "woman question" and a women's suffrage referendum on the 1874 ballot. Given the controversial nature of this topic, as a young girl Helga inevitably overheard conversations on what rights women should have in America. Although the ballot failed at the state level, the vote from the town of Manistee, and the local editorials showed support for the amendment. The failure led to strong determination by local women to "fight out this battle with a zeal that shall know no discouragement, a courage that shall never tire." They invited Susan B. Anthony and Elizabeth Cady Stanton to lecture. In a town this small, their visits introduced Helga to the importance of women's rights.[2]

But something far more important affected Helga directly. At only fifteen, she discovered she was preg-

Helga's mother, Karen Hendriksdatter Johanssen, was widowed when Helga was only two years old. Helga's stepfather, a merchant with the surname Haug, brought the family to Manistee, Michigan, when Helga was eleven.

Photo circa 1870s, Courtesy Portch/Bahr Family Photograph Collection.

MILLER [monogram] MINNEAPOLIS, MINN.

nant and her life changed dramatically. In Norway, young women from the rural farmlands sometimes became pregnant before marriage without disgrace, but it usually led to a marriage with the father of the child. However, Helga was not a rural farm girl living in Norway; she was the stepdaughter and only child of an immigrant merchant living in America. Circumstances surrounding the fifteen-year-old's pregnancy remain mysterious. She may have been raped while working as a maid in a wealthy home, or an irresponsible father walked away when she became pregnant, or perhaps she entered a relationship with a man her family did not approve of for religious, ethnic, or character reasons and they intervened. No one knows. What is known is this unplanned pregnancy radically altered Helga's future.

On October 12, 1876, sixteen-year-old Helga married Ole Estby, a twenty-eight-year-old non-English speaking immigrant from Grue Solor, Norway, who had arrived in America in 1873. He worked in logging camps near Manistee, Michigan, although he initially trained as a carpenter in Germany.[3] Grue Solor is the same region her stepfather came from in Norway, so they likely knew each other earlier. Her marriage to Ole, a Norwegian bachelor, seemed arranged to solve a family problem and avoid shame. Helga gave birth to a daughter she named Clara on November 26, and Ole Estby was probably not the father of her child.[4]

Soon after their marriage, Ole and Helga joined the quest of many Norwegian immigrants who had been drawn to this country by the promise of free land. They started their new life together homesteading in Yellow Medicine County near Canby, Minnesota. Within one year of young Helga's life, she became a wife, a mother, and a pioneer homesteader on the barren prairies near the Minnesota-Dakota border. After their move west, Helga and Ole presented Clara as the child of their own marriage. This family secret was a fiction that Helga and Ole maintained until Clara became a young adult.[5]

For a child raised in the cosmopolitan city of Christiana and during the boom times of Manistee, Michigan, the new challenges of motherhood and farming in an isolated prairie must have been daunting. As she left her family and home and drove off in a Conestoga wagon with her new husband and infant daughter, Clara, she likely had mixed feelings. She may have been enamored with "Western fever" like so many land-poor Norwegian immigrants, lured with the promise of potential riches for homesteaders, and grateful for the marriage with Ole that gave her and her daughter respectability. Or the sudden turn of events in her life may have left her feeling desolate and scared.

Her husband surely saw his future success linked to settling a 160-acre homestead, a general belief confirmed in many letters sent back to Norway by friends and relatives who had immigrated to the United States. The fervency of these American letters

Similar to this farm family, Helga and Ole lived in a one-room sod home on the Minnesota prairie near Canby.

enticed Norwegians to leave their families and venture to America, a migration so great that by the early twentieth century, Norway lost as many citizens as had comprised her total population in 1800.[6]

The Estbys were among the early settlers to Canby; the first had arrived only five years earlier in 1872 after the end of the Sioux War. Their farmland was about seven miles north of the city of Canby, a city populated in 1877 primarily by Norwegians. It offered a community where Ole could feel at home with his limited knowledge of English.

Although Yellow Medicine County promised fertile land, grasshoppers had devoured farmers' crops for the past four years, causing many bankrupt farmers to abandon their homesteads and their dreams. It proved fortuitous, however, that the young Estby family filed in 1877, a year before the infestation ended and a large influx of immigrants arrived. This likely reinforced young Helga's trust in risk taking as a way to solve problems.

Helga and Ole arrived in a land bereft of trees. They could see miles and miles of high-grass prairie, with cottonwood and ash trees found only along the river. A vast expanse of sky and land prevailed with nothing to break the wind. Coming from Norway and then Manistee, which nestled near the shores and forests of Lake Michigan, it was a dramatic geographic shift. With no seas, no nearby lakes, no forests, and no mountains, they saw none of the familiar landmarks etched in their memories of earlier days in Norway or Michigan. On the Canby prairie in the 1870s, pioneers battled the wind that at times blew like a cyclone, a sweeping wind that Helga could feel coming from miles and miles.

But the prairie soil was rich, with gravel on the kames, which were short ridges formed by accumulated stratified drift from glacier waters. Scattered wetland marshes and ponds drew a multitude of waterfowl such as mallards, commonteals, rails, sand cranes, and Canada geese. Wild raspberries, prairie turnips, prairie peas, and gooseberries provided additional food for settlers.

Because of the wind and the coming winter, Ole and Helga's immediate concern was to build a sod home into one of the kames. They cut three-foot strips of sod from the untilled ground and laid these in brick-like courses, grass-side down. The hillside banked their sod home, a one-room structure with a dirt floor.[7] Most sod dwellings provided very little light or air in the poorly ventilated rooms, often having just one door and window. Compared to the frame and brick homes Helga lived in before, a sod home was a crude construction that proved difficult to maintain. It offered inexpensive housing, however, which usually lasted three to five years.

Helga, like other pioneer prairie wives, fought a constant battle against pests, including prairie dogs and snakes that came through the dirt floor in spring. To keep the house clean, sheets draped under the sod roof caught the dirt and bugs. Rivulets of mud ran through the dwellings when rain soaked the sod. A fastidious housekeeper, who often said, "The cheapest thing in the world is a five-cent cake of soap," Helga found housekeeping in her sod house conditions a continual challenge.[8]

These early years brought the loss of one child at birth, a firstborn son they named Ole.[9] During the next few years, Helga was continually pregnant or nursing a newborn. Their son Olaf was born in March, 1879, the

Two of Helga and Ole's children, Bertha and Olaf, in the mid-1880s. Helga was an excellent seamstress and lacemaker and most likely had sewn these clothes.

Courtesy Portch/Bahr Family Photograph Collection.

couple's first daughter Ida in September, 1880, and another daughter, Hedwig (called Bertha), in March, 1882. Without even a two-year span between births, she bore another son, Henry, in January, 1884, and one more son, Arthur, in November, 1885.[10]

Birthing, nursing, and raising these six young children and keeping a sod home livable were only part of Helga's responsibilities for survival on the frontier. Settling a home in this demanding environment required women to be physically and emotionally strong. Rather than a city neighborhood with friends next door, now Helga had only herself and family to rely on. Never-ending work and long distances between farms made close friendships and regular socialization with neighborhood women almost nonexistent. Because they lived in such isolation, they seldom mingled with anybody, and the family and children spoke in Norwegian because of Ole's lack of English.[11]

As a farm wife, Helga's days involved constant chores—churning butter, making soap, sewing, mending and patching clothes, planting, weeding, harvesting and preserving garden produce, making tallow candles, or cleaning kerosene lamps. During her childhood in Norway and America, Helga developed exceptional skills as a seamstress. But having been an urban child, the challenges of homestead farming were all new to her.

The ability of the homemaker to make the most of the environment determined the subsistence level of the family. Western homesteading women knew their resourcefulness and hard work were essential, and they received respect as the nurturers and center of all life around the early farms. As the character Ántonia tells Jim in Willa Cather's book on prairie life, *My Ántonia*, "We'd never have got through if I hadn't been so strong. I've always had good health, thank God, and I was able to help him in the fields until right up to the time my babies came."[12]

Prairie reminiscences from women settlers also spoke of genuine satisfactions. Many mentioned they liked the idea of the family working together, and they took pride in being a real helpmate to their husbands. Pleasures needed to be simple. As one pioneer stated, "You have to respect each other and work together .... Joy was found in small things like a child's first step, playing games .... Good crops, or a root cellar filled with canned goods and produce for the coming winter months gave great satisfaction."[13] For immigrants with meager resources available to them in Norway, the bounty in America seemed far more promising than anything in their homeland. This may have been particularly true for Ole. Optimism prevailed; the hard work and fierce determination required of frontier homesteaders would surely be rewarded.

During these years, Helga gained a sense of her importance and worth to her growing family. Although the sudden move from her merchant city family into the role of marginal homesteader must have been daunting, the family did make progress economically as indicated by the house and outbuildings they eventually built on their homestead. However, she might have identified more with Beret, the prairie wife in the well-known Norwegian novel *Giants in the Earth*. This Norwegian-American writer, O. E. Rolvaag, recognized that early life on the prairie in North Dakota was not a place of sustenance for all women. Instead, they often suffered from severe isolation and loneliness because of living so remotely from friends and neighbors, unlike the settlers in Central Minnesota where woods and lakes and villages offered more variety and community.

In Rolvaag's book, the first of a trilogy on a Norwegian immigrant settlement in the Dakota prairie not far from Yellow Medicine County, the wife of Per Hansa lives in conflict with the prairie. Sometimes seen as a powerful, omnipresent, and malevolent force shaping their lives, the prairie imposed a severe trial or testing for the pioneers. As Rolvaag wrote: "Beret sees her transportation to Dakota Territory as punishment for her sin of conceiving a child out of wedlock. The prairie is the instrument to effect punishment and Beret is tested by her Creator in the crucible of the prairie."[14]

Which was it for Helga? The Minnesota experience gave her a place where she might have surmounted the challenges with the immigrant settler's optimism that these were temporary difficulties, worthy of enduring to improve the family's fortunes. Or was she a young displaced Americanized city woman identifying more with Beret's feelings? Perhaps both were true. Helga's next actions demonstrated that the simple pleasures of a full root cellar and smiling child were clearly not enough for her.

3
THE CRUCIBLE YEARS

My mother was afraid of tornadoes and cyclones.
She wanted to come where we would be safe.

—IDA ESTBY, DAUGHTER

If the isolation of the prairie distressed Helga, the Siberian-like winter of 1880–81 severely tested her emotional health. The summer of 1880 led to the harvest of an excellent crop and the county again became known as the "land of promise." But heavy and frequent rains in August made it impossible to begin stacking on most farms near Canby until the middle of September, right when Helga gave birth to Ida on September 18.

Just in the midst of threshing, a major unexpected snowstorm started the worst winter of the century, far before farmers had taken their crops to the granaries. In historical accounts of Canby, no winter has compared to this one in duration, continued severity, depth of snow, and damage to property.[1] When darkness came on the evening of Friday, October 15, Helga and Ole saw an occasional flake of snow, but by midnight the wind and snow increased in fury. On Saturday, a blizzard raged with such violence that no farmers dared venture outside their sod homes, even to feed the animals. The fury continued until Monday afternoon, October 18. Snow banks in the city of Canby piled up almost level with second story windows, and snowdrifts filled Main Street from ten to fifteen feet deep. Many a farmer was compelled to dig down several feet to get to the barn door and it required one's best endeavors to keep cattle from starving or suffocating. No preparations had been made for such a storm and great numbers of stock perished.[2]

Frightened families experienced weeks of terror. When the wood and coal supply vanished, farmers relied on hay, fence posts, and grain for fuel to keep from freezing to death. Snow completely buried many of the claim shanties in the country. Blizzard followed blizzard and prairie winds created drifts ten to fifteen feet deep. Pioneers excavated tunnels from the house to the barn, to the woodpile, and to the wells. If Ole or Helga ventured outside these paths, drifts like quicksand could suck them and their farm animals to their deaths because the soft deep snow was impossible to walk through.[3] By December, no groceries or provisions remained in the stores. The railway in Yellow Medicine County was blocked for weeks at a time, virtually shutting off the region from receiving any help, or even delivery of outside newspapers and mail. Helga, Ole, their two young children, and infant

Ida spent long weeks of discouraging isolation in the midst of these dangerous surroundings. If their provisions didn't hold until the railroad reopened, famine was a real threat. Some lost their lives in the storms or suffered frostbite and, as a result, amputated limbs.

Yet, during these dreary circumstances, the Scandinavian prairie settlers showed their grit and determination. Volunteers began to shovel snow off the railroad tracks, businesses reopened by creating tunnels to their doors, and local theater groups formed to relieve the monotony of the siege. The railroad company gave permission to cut and use the snow fences along the track for fuel.[4] How did Helga and Ole, huddled alone in their sod home with their family and newborn, cope during this devastating winter? Whatever tenacity it took, Ole and Helga endured. When summer crops proved bountiful in the county the following year, the family's pioneer perseverance was rewarded.

Living in the era before readily available birth control, Helga's continual pregnancies suggest she adopted similar cultural values as other Norwegian immigrant farm pioneers. Although women gathered together occasionally at husking bees, quilting bees, and other work-related activities, their daily lives were often very lonely. Also, these reserved Norwegian wives in Minnesota did not ordinarily discuss personal, intimate concerns. Most women followed traditional religious teachings that reinforced feminine virtues to be supporting and nurturing. This included that their role was to satisfy their husband's natural sexual desires and to bear children. This view of marriage was understood and rarely questioned.[5]

Once sixteen-year-old Helga married Ole and bore his children, she invested all of her considerable energy and talent working alongside her husband to create a sustainable and loving family life. Motherhood also aroused in Helga a sense of protectiveness. Especially after the frightening winter of 1880, living on their remote prairie land began to raise fears for the safety of the children she loved.

As a young mother in Minnesota in the 1880s, Helga faced another fear, particularly ominous because of its invisibility. Parents could recognize a treacherous snowstorm, a raging prairie fire, or a cyclone funnel, and seek a safe shelter for their children. But when Minnesota towns and surrounding farm homes experienced virulent outbreaks of diphtheria, this highly contagious disease caused significant alarm. Doctors found themselves helpless to treat diphtheria when it attacked families in its worse form known as "black diphtheria." The lack of specific knowledge of the cause, or of any preventative or curative agents, staggered both doctors and laymen. Although light cases could be cured, the more deadly black diphtheria caused death "with startling certainty and machine-like regularity…often in a short four days."[6]

Children were particularly vulnerable, suffocating to death as their windpipe closed. Even the finest doctors felt helpless when this attacked a family, and during the epidemics in the 1880s, they saw some parents lose all their children in a matter of days. As parents of young children, the Estby family would be targeted by their local Health Board to receive circulars required by the Minnesota State Board of Health. These disseminated the latest information concerning the restriction and prevention of diphtheria. Some of the information in this 1880 bulletin would later be disputed, but it provided the best medical insight of the era.[7]

Helga and Ole read that as a contagious and infectious disease, diphtheria proved most fatal when found in filthy localities. "These common and visible forms of filth are seen in the untidiness of living and sleeping rooms, in the filthy condition of clothing and persons, in decaying garbage in cellars, in the faulty conditions of cess-pools and privy-vaults."[8] Although this warning placed immense pressure on the housekeeping skills of a family, at least a mother and father could exercise control over these conditions. But the bulletin gave further warnings about the dangerous invisible forms found in drinking water, soil, and odorous gases in drains and sewers. This insidious unseen virus that "is apt to attach itself to clothing, bedding, furniture and be retained for a long time in the walls of the rooms" required that homes receive all the "sunlight possible and a liberal supply of fresh air."[9] Keeping a poorly ventilated sod home in high sanitary conditions was impossible and perhaps prompted the Estbys to build their frame home and outbuildings on the homestead.[10]

Although doctor's experiences showed that even the very neatest families living in commodious homes could suffer as much as those in small squalid hovels, the general perception prevailed that poor housekeeping contributed to a family's tragedy. This added another burden, usually borne by the mother of a home. This opinion also heaped guilt onto the deep grief of losing a child. The Estby family managed to avoid this tragedy that struck some Minnesota communities with as many as eighty to ninety deaths during epidemic stages. But they inevitably carried the anxiety created by these epidemics.

Another burden that dwelled inside each homesteader involved the Estbys directly. If contagious disease epidemics caused an unseen fear for Minnesota farm families, wild prairie fires caused a visible and tangible terror. Fires demanded constant vigilance if farmers hoped to save their homes, barns, grain piles, stock, and livelihood from swift obliteration. But unlike the invisible menace from diphtheria, pioneers knew they could take steps to protect their property by plowing fire breaks and scanning the skies daily for any sign of smoke.

With even a mild wind, fire was treacherous because one never knew where it might start up. And with a bad wind, prairie fires swept everything before it. When sparks flew into the hay, often everything on the farm could be lost. If a fire threatened a home-stead, everyone big enough to help fought the fire. Women often took some old clothing, like a woolen coat dipped in water, and wiped the ground with it, dragging it along the blaze.

In one terror-filled afternoon, Helga fought a fire that came within feet of their home.[11] The Estbys saw signs of the fire raging across the prairie; by the time the suffocating smoke neared their home, the roar and crackle of flames threw sparks high in the air, terrify-ing their livestock and young children. As she needed to help fight the fire, Helga could not comfort their screaming little ones. They managed to save their house and barn—many neighbors were not so lucky and lost their wheat stacks. Worse yet, a farm husband and wife were badly burned from fighting the fire.[12]

After the frightening fire, one final threat convinced Helga they needed to move their growing family off the Minnesota homestead. Sudden and unpredictable cyclones and tornadoes created devastating damage to life and property in Minnesota and pioneers barely had time to flee into the dugouts that every farm needed. In 1885, a tornado hit the Canby area particularly hard.

(following pages) Helga and Ole, around 1887, with six of their chil-dren shortly before selling their prairie homestead in Canby, Min-nesota, and moving to Spokane Falls, Washington Territory.

Courtesy Portch/Bahr Family Photograph Collection.
Detail of this photograph on page 30.

The Estbys felt the same fear as their neighbors felt on "Black Friday," the name given to a frightening storm on June 19, 1885. Near sundown, Helga looked on the horizon and saw a dark cloud roll in from the west. Within minutes, it began to rain in torrents and hailstones struck with the force of bullets, with a sound compared to "a continuous fire of musketry." Glass, windows, storefronts, and window lights were shattered into fragments. Nearby barns blew down and hail the size of hen's eggs knocked bark off the trees. Within an hour and a half, twelve to eighteen inches of water covered the prairie, causing extensive damage to crops and trees. After the storm, Helga learned that the severe winds, hail storms, and falling trees had killed a young child and a baby in his mother's arms as they tried to get to shelter—exactly the fear that Helga harbored.[13]

Just one month later, on July 16, another major storm caused havoc seven miles northwest of Canby, very near the Estby homestead. In a three-mile destructive sweep, a new barn was blown flat, another barn almost full of hay was lifted off its foundations, a falling tree killed a man, a barn struck by lightning burned down and killed two horses, lightning caused three houses to be consumed by fire, game was killed in great abundance, and most growing crops were greatly injured by the storm.[14]

That was enough for Helga and Ole. Scared of future tornadoes and cyclones, the Estbys began planning a move to the West, a region promoted actively by the Northern Pacific Railroad. The assurances in brochures of a better climate, available land, affordable housing, and educational opportunities in "the promised land" lured many an immigrant to the West. So many immigrants came in the 1880s, they established a vibrant Scandinavian presence in churches and organizations in urban centers in Washington State, such as Seattle, Tacoma, and Spokane Falls, the new "gem" city of the Pacific Northwest. One brochure particularly addressed the quality of educated people who lived in Spokane Falls and the educational opportunities for children, a topic that would have drawn Helga's attention. Educated in America, and fluent both in written and spoken English and Norwegian, she had more schooling than many of the Scandinavian farm women. She longed for her children to have the chance to better themselves in every way, intellectually, spiritually, and materially.[15] In the Canby region, she saw that young girls often began working for families instead of attending high school. The brochure boasted: "The permanent population of Spokane Falls is of a very highly intellectual and moral character…. They recognize the fact that intellectual culture is the genius of the age in which we live, and constitutes in itself a true exponent of wealth and power."[16]

The brochure then elaborated on the new public schools and the superintendent of education with a doctorate, the high school literary society, the two private schools, the establishment of Gonzaga University (a Jesuit institution), the four-year Spokane College and the Methodist-Episcopal College, which aimed to "provide thorough scholarship and a high standard of moral and Christian character." All three colleges insisted they offered education equal to those of the East and included modern languages, Latin, Greek, philosophy, higher math, logic, and bookkeeping in their curricula. For Helga, familiar with urban life, a city that grew from less than three hundred to more than two thousand in just thirty months must have sounded remarkable. Spokane Falls offered churches, newspapers, an opera house, good hotels and a high percentage of college-educated citizens.[17]

What most likely precipitated their final decision was a September 21, 1886, newspaper from Spokane, Washington, that caught their eye, especially an advertisement for twenty-five carpenters wanted to work for $3.50 a day on the Spokane and Idaho Railroad.[18] Tired of the drudgery and unpredictability of farming, with a young wife frightened to live on the prairie, Ole likely found this new option to practice his original trade appealing. It was enough enticement to get the Estbys to join the vast group of Norwegians and other immigrants who participated in the "second migration" to the Northwest, a movement that grew to more than 150,000 Scandinavians in the Pacific Northwest between 1890 and 1910.[19] Eager to move, the Estbys sold their house and land for $1000, and Ole moved West. As soon as their six children recovered from the measles, Helga, now twenty-seven (and two months pregnant), and the children boarded the train in May of 1887 to join Ole.

After the challenges of eleven years of homesteading on the prairie, the young wife and mother emerged a very different woman than the young bride who moved to Minnesota with her infant child. Through the hardships of isolation, mercurial crop production, the worst snowstorm of the century, and threats of fire, cyclones, and pestilence, she not only endured but also helped her carpenter husband carve out a living on the farm. She birthed and nurtured six healthy children, grieved the loss of their firstborn son, and built a farm, which left them with modest funds to choose a new destiny as a family. She knew during every day of her work that she was needed, essential to their family's quality of life.

These formative years gave Helga an inner confidence of her ingenuity, persistence, adaptability, survival skills, intelligence, and talents. Though glad to leave, like many other pioneer women, she took with her permanent qualities of character forged in the crucible of prairie survival. And when she moved to Spokane Falls, the 1888 city directory listed her with the title she chose: She did not identify herself as housewife but as Helga Estby, "farmer."[20] Yet nothing in Helga's imagination prepared her for the twist of fate that befell her on a dark Spokane Falls street just one year later.

4 SURPRISES IN SPOKANE FALLS

*I also suffered much pain at all times and much
worry, loss of sleep, and nervous prostration.*

—HELGA ESTBY'S TESTIMONY
SPOKANE COUNTY COURT RECORDS

One of the first sights and sounds Helga and
the children witnessed when they stepped off the train
in May of 1887 was the roaring, spectacular Spokane
Falls. The Spokane River cascaded over upper and
lower basalt channels in 130 feet of stunning power
right in the heart of downtown. The pride of early settlers, it was the source that sparked imaginative men
in the early 1880s to gamble their destinies on this isolated land even though it was far from any railroad
connections. Minneapolis had gained status as the
largest flour manufacturing center of the world
through the 20,000 horse power generated from the
famed St. Anthony's Falls, yet engineers estimated the
power of Spokane Falls at a monumental 90,000
horse power.[1] This power motivated pioneers to tame
nature and harness the water to run the early granaries, lumber mills, and other industries.

The Spokane Indians knew this magnificent resource as the home for rich runs of spring salmon, which drew the tribal members back to their traditional river waters each August. For many Spokane Falls citizens and visitors, the falls' roaring presence near the dusty dirt streets of the city spoke of a greater power, a Creator with a lavish spirit of energy that refreshed; people constantly paused on the bridges to watch the foaming swirls and hear this thundering natural force. The one-hundred-mile Spokane River cut a swath through eastern Washington territory from the north end of Coeur d'Alene Lake to its confluence with the Columbia River below Fort Spokane. Each natural wonder added to a sense of the splendor of the Northwest, a visual feast to Helga after the flat expanse of the prairie.

For centuries, this region along the river had been the ancestral home of the Spokane Indians, most commonly translated as "children of the sun." An interior Salish tribe, they lived in the general area of the Spokane River in three primary bands, the Upper Spokanes, the Middle Spokanes, and the Lower Spokanes. They began fur trading with the first white men in 1810. Both Protestant and Catholic missionaries came into the area during the ensuing years, but it was not until the 1860s that miners and farmers began their push to settle in the Spokane tribal lands. The Northern Pacific Railroad arrived in Spokane in 1881, which opened up the territory to easy access for settlers; that same year, the Lower Spokanes moved to the newly established Spokane Reservation. By 1887, when Ole and Helga came to Spokane Falls, the Upper and Middle Spokanes ceded titles to their lands and many moved to the Coeur d'Alene Reservation.[2]

The other sound that promised growth and prosperity to settlers' ears was the constant chugging from the transcontinental railroads. By the time the Estbys arrived, railroads going east to Coeur d'Alene led to the rich mining areas, routes going north led to Colville and Canada for lumber and mining, and routes going south led to the Palouse, a land renowned for exceptionally fertile wheat fields. Now, instead of waking up in relative isolation, Helga woke to the bustle of a city brimming with optimism and reckless hope. Within one month, she and Ole purchased three lots just one block east of Division Street on Pine and Fourth Streets. Southeast of the heart of the business district, this location was the same one advertised in the *Spokane Chronicle* they had seen earlier in Minnesota. Helga's choice to list herself as a farmer, not a housewife, in the 1888 city census suggests she may have started a garden farm on these lots and had plans to sell produce in the city. For the first time in their lives, they lived in a non-Norwegian community. Spokane Falls included a large English colony, and many Scotsmen, Irishmen, Canadians, and Germans were numbered among the leading businessmen of the city. Helga also made a key decision affecting the fate of her family. For Ole and the children, learning English now seemed essential. Helga no longer allowed Norwegian to be spoken in

Howard Street, Spokane, in 1887, the year the Estbys arrived from Minnesota, with a large "Welcome" sign for new settlers.

their home, primarily so Ole could learn faster. As a carpenter, he needed to be capable of making and signing contracts in English. Their family even began attending an English-speaking church, rather than joining the congregation that worshiped in Norwegian. The children adapted quickly and felt confident in their language abilities within a short time.[3]

The city sponsored its first fair where citizens proudly displayed homegrown flowers, fruits and vegetables, embroidery, quilts, rag rugs, and knitting. Helga had learned to do beautiful handiwork as a child in Norway, so she began entering her creations and earned many prizes.[4]

Helga found pleasure in showing her children the sights of the lively city, reminiscent of her own childhood days in Christiana, Norway. Walking along the handsome brick blocks of magnificent stores, they could look into the large plate-glass windows. There they viewed the fine dry goods, silks, satins, jewelry, hardware, furniture, and rugs offered to fashionably dress and furnish the homes in Spokane Falls' growing population of affluent citizens. Sometimes she even took the older children for a longer walk over to the beautiful Browne's Addition neighborhood. During Spokane's gilded age, she saw the elegant mansions being built by men who had gained enormous wealth from the mining, lumber, and business boom. No expense seemed too much for some of these homes as owners brought in marble from Europe, fine woods from Asia, or chandeliers and clocks from Tiffany's in New York. Even if living in these homes seemed unimaginable, she appreciated that these same wealthy citizens encouraged the flourishing of live theater and local musical productions, like *Pinafore* and *Mikado*—something that every citizen could enjoy.

But rapid growth came at a cost, one that proved particularly painful for the happiness and peace of the Estby family. When they arrived in 1887, there were around six thousand people; within three years the city claimed a population of twenty thousand.[5] With such rapid growth, the city failed to keep up a healthy infrastructure. Sanitary conditions were marginal with fetid cesspools polluting the alleys. Wood boardwalks lined the central dirt roads of commerce and often the city failed to repair the dangerous holes caused by cattle drives, creating hazards for unsuspecting people or animals.[6]

What happened to Helga on a dark night in 1888 near Riverside Avenue and Division Street shattered whatever burgeoning confidence the couple had in trusting their own strength to carve out a better life. Riverside Avenue, a major thoroughfare, was being repaired and graded, and no markers existed alerting pedestrians to the dangers this created. While hurrying home one night, Helga's foot hit an obstacle, and she fell hard on piles of rocks and deeply injured her pelvic area.

This fall caused serious health problems that debilitated Helga and tumbled her into despair.[7] When time revealed the extent of her injuries and lingering illness, Helga decided to take an unusual step. Because she no longer could contribute to the needs of her family, she sued the city of Spokane Falls for $5000 for failure to provide warning signs or barriers for pedestrians.[8] This meant Helga needed to appear before an all-male legal system to speak publicly about extremely private feminine health issues. Remnants of the Victorian emphasis on separate spheres for men and women still remained; Helga's decision to enter the public realm of the courtroom where the judge, lawyers, and jurors were all men showed unusual fortitude. Her refusal to remain invisible and silent on the effects of a public event on her private domestic life clearly countered prevailing custom.[9] It was so unusual for women to testify in court, that their public presence often caused a sensation. Although her original testimony is not recorded, she described her 1888 injuries in a later deposition:

> I fell on Riverside Avenue, near Division Street, in the City of Spokane, and struck upon the rocks. The fall was upon my pelvic region in front and caused the skin to be discolored for a time and muscles to remain sore for a long time. There was also some slight injury to my left leg. As a result of the fall the internal walls of the pelvic region and the womb became very sore, particularly at the time of my periodic sickness, resulting in an abnormal hemorrhage at such times and also caused an abnormal duration of such sickness. I also suffered much pain at all times and much loss of sleep, worry, and nervous prostration. The pain also at times caused fainting spells.[10]

During these months Helga was often under the care of doctors and nurses. Once physically strong, Helga now lived in chronic pain, weakened and anemic from the injuries.

In a trial that lasted for several days during February, 1889, seventeen witnesses testified on Helga's behalf. One of the witnesses, Dr. Mary Latham, practicing in the relatively new field of gynecology, had come to Spokane in 1887. One of the first female graduates of the Cincinnati College of Medicine and

Surgery, Latham was known for her expertise in women's and children's diseases, and her testimony on the extent of Helga's injuries likely aided the case.[11]

The city vehemently argued against the suit, trying to either pass the blame onto Helga for not being careful enough or onto the company hired to do the grading. Helga stood in front of these men and spoke directly about the personal injuries to her internal organs, the frightening side effects, and the discouraging struggle in trying to mother seven children while in ill health. Such a large family needed a mother's strength and talents for their livelihood; now a heavy burden was placed on her oldest daughter, eleven-year-old Clara.

One month before the trial, on January 29, 1889, the Estbys needed to borrow $60 on their city lots, perhaps for court expenses.[12] A February 21, 1889, *Spokane Falls Review* headline announced the outcome of Helga's bold lawsuit: "The Jury in the Estley [*sic*] Suit Against the City Failed to Agree."[13] After risking public exposure of her personal life, Helga must have been quite depressed by the hung jury. Shortly thereafter, Ole and Helga satisfied the $60 debt and borrowed another $250 mortgage on their city land, perhaps for more medical or attorney's bills.[14] Her attorney appealed and the case came to court again in July, 1889 and the next jury found in Helga's favor. The jury awarded her a judgment of $2500 plus $600 for court costs.[15] Although small compensation for loss of health, even after attorney fees it provided a princely sum for a large family with a lifetime of marginal resources. Equally important was the affirmation Helga experienced that reinforced her choice to test and trust the public world of American law. She gained assurance that the American justice system could hear a woman's need and respond fairly. She also saw that defying prevailing convention for women could be rewarded.

The same 1889 summer that saw Helga's lawsuit result in a hung jury, saw devastation come to the prospering frontier town. Around four in the afternoon on Sunday, August 4, when temperatures soared into the 90s, a fire bell clanged the news that a fire had broken out in the middle of town. Helga and Ole heard the fire alarm from their Fourth Avenue home and climbed with their children up to a lean-to roof above their laundry and utility room. At first, they were not concerned because, unlike when wildfires roared across dry prairie lands, Spokane Falls prided itself on an excellent fire department with immediate access to an unlimited supply of water from the river downtown. Within minutes, the horse-drawn fire engine and Volunteer Fire Department members rushed to the scene, joined by many citizens eager to help.

The fire department, however, could not stop the small fire and a scatter of shanties north of Railroad Avenue quickly picked up the flying sparks. Within minutes, when firefighters failed to get sufficient water pressure from the pumps, the Estbys watched in disbelief as a wall of flame poured northward toward First Avenue. Panicked citizens rushed away from the exploding flames, running toward Fourth Avenue where the Estbys lived. "We watched the people go by with all their belongings that they could collect in sheets and they carried bird carriages and little dogs and little cats and whole families going by," recalled Ida, who watched from the roof with her family when she was six years old.[16]

Though the fire did not come up as far as their street, by midnight over thirty-two blocks of the nearby business district lay in ruins. Exquisite buildings, including the new four-story Spokane Opera House, first-class hotels, banks, and businesses were reduced to ashes. The gem city suffered a loss to buildings totaling over ten million dollars and by morning was a visual wasteland of destruction, except for the Crescent block. Helga lost the illusion of security the river had given her as a protection from fires. Seeing this fiery devastation so close to her family left Helga with a new uneasiness and anxiety, reminiscent of her panic after their prairie fire.

By August 6, relief supplies began arriving by trains and a tent city sprang up overnight in Spokane Falls, encouraged by the generous outpouring from other parts of the country. Though the city lay in ashes, the Estbys saw an astonishing surge of fortitude and creativity as the city leaders chose to see the fire as an opportunity to rebuild the city of their dreams. Commerce in the tent city revived immediately, and Helga decided to show the children the businessmen's creative temporary solutions. "There was the Grahams and Libby Photography and the Davenport and they were all in tents," recalled daughter Ida, remembering Spokane after the 1889 fire. "I can remember mother took us down to see all the tents and everything." Because Helga seldom allowed the children to go to town, especially when she was ill, this seemed like a real treat.[17]

For Ole, this city crisis provided immediate opportunities for him, along with steady wages that lasted well into the next two years. The city leaders were determined to still host the planned Exposition of 1890 and built the new structures with fireproof granite. The Estby family benefited from their commitment.

Something else proved fortunate for Helga. New breakthroughs in the controversial field of gynecology were occurring and three surgeons operated on her.[18] During a long convalescent period afterward, Clara, as oldest daughter, became her mother's main source of help in the home. A thoughtful and responsible child, Clara was now fourteen years old, capable of getting children ready for school, cooking family meals, and providing comfort to her mother. Best of all, a few months after the successful surgery, Helga regained her health. She no longer lived with the belief she would be weak and painridden forever. After a rare five-year pause between births, Helga became pregnant with their eighth child and gave birth to William in April, 1892. With this renewal in their fortunes and the children growing, Helga began to dream a new dream.

5 FRONTIER VICES AND THE MOVE TO MICA CREEK

*We used to have lots of fun, sleigh rides and
hayrides and everything like that.*
—IDA ESTBY, DAUGHTER

None of the glowing publicity enticing new-comers to Spokane Falls acknowledged the rawer side of the city beyond the elegant Victorian homes, cultural entertainment, and a conservative, highly educated populace. Helga soon realized that the Spokane Falls of the late 1880s and early 1890s seemed more like two cities, a town with a split personality. The town leadership encouraged the emphasis on churches, libraries, schools, colleges, and literary societies, while simultaneously catering to a large population of transient men. They allowed what westerners called an "open" town, a description determined by how strictly police enforced laws against prostitution, gambling, and alcohol.

The growing city included many self-employed craftsmen like Ole, working men who planned to set roots in the community and raise their families.

Known as "homeguards," they often joined the early unions, wanting to better their lives. However, another large group of men were known by locals as "blanket stiffs," including seasonal miners, loggers, and ranch and farm hands.[1] These men lived a migrant lifestyle, constantly on the move looking for better jobs offering good pay or new adventures. Now that the railroads in Spokane Falls provided a means of national distribution, companies hired these men primarily for their muscles to help extract the vast resources of timber, grain, and ore.[2]

Although Spokane Falls was becoming known for beautiful residential neighborhoods, these were not the neighborhoods in the Estby's backyard. Within a few short city blocks from their home existed all the lures of a brawling western town, created by greedy businessmen for workers passing through. The city catered extensively to the drinking, sexual, gambling, and entertainment desires of the hungry miners, loggers, and farm hands carrying cash to spend. Saloons, gambling halls, boarding houses, billiard halls, Turkish baths, Chinese opium dens, and brothels openly

operated in a downtown area that reached over to Division Street. The Estby home on Pine Street was just one block east and a few blocks north of the active downtown. Although city ordinances outlawed prostitution in 1889, the police department, under the orders of the city council, was lax in how they enforced the antiprostitution laws. Instead of eliminating prostitution in the city, these laws allowed the city to collect fines systematically—rich revenue for the city coffers. Once a month, prostitutes came to city hall to pay their fees.[3] Nor was there only one identified red-light district; rather, these places were scattered throughout town, with some not too far from Helga's home. A prostitution hierarchy existed, with the lowest-ranking working in "cribs," which were easily observable small shacks built in city alleys.

A prevailing frame of mind justified allowing the vice-regulation policies of the city. Some city leaders believed that the prostitute was a necessary guardian of virtue who kept innocent moral women from being raped and ruined by men fulfilling their natural sexual needs. This doctrine of sexual necessity, supported by some medical physicians into the 1910s, asserted that men periodically needed to obtain sexual release for their health's sake.[4] "We could do it; it is within our power to drive those women out," admitted Spokane's mayor to inquisitors who questioned the city's open policies. "But, speaking frankly, I question the advisability of doing it. Reputable physicians say the social evil is a necessary evil—that without it the number of shocking crimes would increase greatly."[5]

By 1890, the oldest children in the Estby family were nearing their teenage years and inevitably needed to walk through the rough edges of the city to attend school, visit friends, or go shopping. Even if the Estbys could prevent their children from wandering into back alleys and encountering prostitution cribs, Spokane Falls' lively street corners fascinated them. Palmistry readers, Chinese grocery-cart peddlers, "fire-and-brimstone" preachers, tinhorn street gamblers, and clairvoyant mediums all sang their songs of invitation. Drunken men and vagrants commonly loitered or roamed the streets and violence and disorder could erupt any night—hardly the ideal environment that the Estbys desired.

Helga's nervousness in having the children out on these streets caused her to restrict the children's activities outside the house, becoming extra protective as she worried over their moral and physical well-being.[6] When she first came to Spokane Falls, Helga also brought her Midwest settler's prejudice about Native Americans with her, an anxiety she passed on to her children. Peaceful Indians from the Spokane Tribe often came to the city, and Helga hired an Indian woman to help wash clothes in their yard. However, the children were "deathly afraid of her," and Helga kept them indoors during the wash-woman's visits.[7] One day, while six of the children were walking in the city streets, a large Indian chief, dressed in paint and wearing feathers, noticed a glass-bead necklace that Clara was wearing. Interested in this jewelry, he reached out to touch it, and the family assumed he wanted to grab Clara. All the children screamed. Speaking in English, he assured them he wasn't going to take her. He just wanted "to pat the pretty beads."[8] But in Helga's eyes, the former farm children's primary source of vulnerability came from their lack of experience in living in an unpredictable urban environment.

Although Helga appreciated the benefits of the city, the open city's flagrant problems contributed to her desire to return to the countryside where she perceived a simpler and more moral life prevailed. She knew her growing children needed to be free to roam and explore without her constant worry about corruptive influences. Restless once again, the family began to think about moving outside the city, but near enough to be accessible to the advantages of Spokane. About this time, only twenty-eight miles southeast of Spokane Falls, the small town of Rockford actively encouraged settlers to come to the beautiful Rock Creek Valley. Rich agricultural farmland, situated near the foothills of the Coeur d'Alene mountain range, was available through the railroads and government. In 1892, Helga and Ole paid $600 to the Northern Pacific Railroad for 160 acres in Mica Creek, a Scandinavian enclave of farms known as "Little Norway." Their funds most likely came from money seeded in their two apparent misfortunes: the town's fire and Helga's fall.[9] Once again their family enjoyed the comfort of rural values in a Scandinavian community and the freedom and fresh air of the countryside.

Helga, now thirty-two, finally found a place where she believed their children could flourish. She took pride in Ole's carpentry skills when he built an attractive three-bedroom farmhouse and pine furnishings. Two bedrooms upstairs gave the boys and the girls separate spaces. Clara, Ida, Bertha, and later, baby Lillian, shared one room and the five brothers, Olaf, Johnny, Arthur, William, and Henry shared the other. Ole and Helga finally had a private bedroom and a dining room on the main floor.

It made the constant work of taking care of her family far easier than their days living on the remote Minnesota prairie. A nearby pump provided easy access to natural spring water. Ole added an all-purpose building and furnished it with an old wood cook stove for heating water. Here Helga washed clothes and gave the children summer baths, ground wheat, and dressed chickens and other wild game on a wooden table. Their root cellar stored potatoes and one-gallon crocks that Helga covered with lard in the winter, or filled with cherry and dandelion wine or root beer for the children.

They soon cleared part of the land, planted an orchard and garden, and then built a barn with stalls for horses and small calves, an outbuilding for pigs and

The Estbys enjoyed the wholesome family atmosphere in the small town of Rockford near their Mica Creek farm, like this chilly Fourth of July community celebration at the turn of the century.

cows, and refurbished an old log chicken house that came with the land.[10] For a woman who started raising a family in a one-room dirt-floor sod house on the prairie, this home seemed almost luxurious. Even during hard times, the children could always be fed. Plus, with all the responsibilities in developing the farm and caring for the animals, her children were gaining important work habits. Watching William's and Arthur's delight as they played with their first litter of squealing piglets or remembering Bertha's pride in bringing her father a wildflower bouquet brought Helga a quiet pleasure over their choice to have moved once more.

Although Helga wanted the children to concentrate on English when they moved to Spokane Falls (which gradually changed in name to Spokane in the 1890s), she still desired for them to know the friendship of a Scandinavian community. The Mica Creek neighborhood, with its many Norwegians and Swedish immigrants, had a reputation for common decency, neighborliness, and support during difficult times. Even better, these Scandinavians knew how to have fun. In Minnesota, many of the religious Norwegians came from the "Haugian" Lutheran faith background, part of an earlier pietistic revival movement in rural Norway in the 1800s. One outgrowth of this movement included a legalism that deemed certain actions sinful and made some Norwegians fearful of life's simple pleasures. But in Mica Creek, their neighbors visited for card games, sleigh rides and hayrides, and Ole could drink his daily beer without criticism from the community. "We used to have lots of fun," recalled daughter Ida.[11] Nor did Helga feel the isolation that permeated her days on the prairie in Minnesota.

The local community around Mica Creek, centered in school and family life, offered rich everyday moments. The schoolhouse became the neighborhood gathering place for harvest dances, box socials, a literary club, baseball games, eighth-grade certification days, pie socials, fairs, and the election polling place. The school was right near the Estby's land, allowing the family convenient access to school-sponsored social events. Helga appreciated that their Mica Creek community placed a high value on education for daughters. At times, more girls attended the Mica Creek schoolhouse than boys because families needed boys at home for clearing land, planting and harvesting crops, cutting wood, or tending livestock.[12] When daughters outgrew the eighth-grade local schools, many families encouraged them to attend high school in the city, where they often worked as maids in exchange for room and board. This practice allowed Clara to attend a Spokane high school.

Beyond their home and fields grew magnificent ponderosa pine forests to wander through, a mountain to lift your eyes and spirit each day, and a mild climate that brought an early spring and a dry summer. The family gathered wildflowers and created bouquets of Indian paintbrush, ladyslippers, bluebells, trilliums, and wild roses to grace their polished handcrafted furnishings. On snowbound wintry evenings, Helga enjoyed crocheting delicate lace for tablecloths, an art she learned as a child in Christiana.

Less protective as a mother now, Helga allowed the older children to take trips to the nearby town of Rockford, a six-mile walk that Olaf especially liked to do.[13] The entire family enjoyed visiting the town's

They shopped at George B. Hurd and Company's General Store, which was kept well stocked for farm family's needs.

general mercantile store where barrels of apples, prunes, apricots, and a showcase full of candy appealed to the children. Hardware supplies, barrels of molasses, and coal oil, as well as the bank in the back of the store, drew in the adults. Helga bought fabrics to sew the children's clothes and enjoyed conversations with local women. Sometimes the family joined the crowd at the train depot waiting for mail delivery, always a favorite event in the city. The trains brought memories of their own adventures riding across the continent from Minnesota.

The Estbys still traveled to Spokane for cultural events. "They had lots of operas and things that would come," recalled daughter Ida. "But that was too expensive for our family because one couldn't go unless we all went." They especially enjoyed seeing live musical performances of the Jessie Shirley Company and theater performances. However, these excursions were extremely rare.[14] Just the train fare for a family of eleven could be prohibitive. Each year though, they did take advantage of the special one-cent-a-mile railway excursion rates aimed to bring surrounding citizens into Spokane to enjoy the annual parades and Fourth-of-July Food Fair. Enticing displays of sun-ripened pears, peaches, cherries, giant squash and potatoes, red-cheeked apples, and wheat and sunflowers encouraged settlers like the Estbys to develop their farms, offering proof of what good earth and hard work could produce.

When the Estbys bought their land in 1892, Ole built their comfortable home and planned to continue making his primary earnings as a carpenter, not as a farmer. He expected to hire out in Rockford, help nearby farmers build barns and outbuildings, or ride the train to work in Spokane. While they built up the farm to meet their family needs, Helga occasionally hired out as a seamstress to augment their incomes.

However, just one year after Ole built their new home, national events shattered the Estby's assumptions about America's ongoing prosperity and their personal ability to keep their farm.

EY CLOSED

hington National and Washin-
ton Savings Banks Sus-
pend Payment.

AS IN GOOD CONDIT

There is Lots of Gold Piled Up
Counters of the Other
Banks.

The suspension of the Bank
kane Falls yesterday was not
its effect upon the other
of the city. Knowing
mercial rela

6 FINANCIAL FEARS AND A FAMILY DEATH

*The children could not understand how the signing
of a piece of paper could change everything, but it
did ... Moor (their mother) was very different. She
went around as if she were carrying a burden.*

—A. RAAEN, GRASS OF THE EARTH

During 1893, Helga traveled away from the
family twice, perhaps to help her mother in Wisconsin
after her stepfather's death. During these months of her
absence, the children wrote affectionate letters to their
mother, using their recently learned English.[1] A long letter
from Ida, now twelve, dated February 9, 1893, let her
mother know of important family events. Ida's reference to
Christy indicates the likelihood of an earlier connection.

> *Dear Mother*
> *I will write a few lines to you and tell you that
> we are all and Will (now 10 months old) is good he
> can stand alone by the wall and he crawls all over
> the floor and puts every thing in his mouth I will tell
> you that my shoes fit me nicely. Henry felt bad*

because he did not get any shoes. Papa bought some overhols for him. It is snowing here to-day. I am waiting for you to come home papa was in Rockford Friday and he bought some Baking powder and we want to invite Richardson's girls on Bertha's Birthday because I had a party on my Birthday and I want her to have some fun on her Birthday because it will not be right to not let her have any fun when I had. I don't feel well today so I can not write good my hand shakes it but I hope you can read it. Bertha wrote so I wanted to write to. My eyes are well now so Clara said that it was no use the glasses. I have nothing more to tell you I will send our regard to you here is a kiss for you I send my love to christy.

> *Your loving Daughter, Ida*

In this same batch of letters, Henry wrote:

> *Dear Mother*
> *I got a pair of overalls papa bought. I had to have Hedvig (Bertha) to write for me I could not write my Self because they was in such a hurry. I will tell you that I'm a good boy all the time you was gone and will help Papa saw wood and put hay in the mangers when he is working with the horses because he is cold. I will tell you that it is snowing up here today. I feed the two little pigs.*
> *Your son, Henry*

Arthur summed up the family feelings when their mama left home when he wrote:

> *Dear Mamma*
> *I want to write a few lines to you but not much. I am a good boy, I stay in the house all the time I will send a kiss to you. I wish you would come home.*
> *Your little boy Arthur Estby*

In another undated letter, Henry wrote:

> *Dear Mamma*
> *I will write a few lines to you, and tell you I am a good boy. I help to cook food for the pig. I send you a kiss. Me and Arthur wrote ours on the same side*
> *Your loving boy,*
> *Henry Estby*

These letters reflect the ways the family coped when their mother needed to be away. They missed her, but took care of one another, whether helping their father with the farm, or remembering the importance of a birthday celebration for a sister and daughter. Helga returned home sometime in the spring, became pregnant again, and then traveled sometime in the late summer, as shown by another similar letter from Bertha and Ida and their Aunt Hanna (Ole's sister) dated September 6, 1893. Helga kept these treasured letters that connected her to her children.

Love and kisses from the children, however, could not solve the reality of a severe financial crash in 1893 that swept the country. In early summer, it hit the heavily mortgaged city of Spokane and directly affected Ole's livelihood. After the 1889 fire devastated the center of Spokane, Dutch financiers had loaned millions of dollars to rebuild the gutted city. The major lenders now reacted with quick and aggressive foreclosures on indebted businesses and individuals.

To the Estby's and the community's shock, within three days of June, seven of the ten Spokane banks failed. Many prominent town leaders lost their real estate to sheriff's sales. Foreclosures affected millions of dollars worth of buildings, choice residential property, commercial sites, and farmlands. This early economic depression in Spokane was described as a period of "gloom and disaster, of crashing banks and crippled industry, of riotous demonstrations and counter organization for law and order."[2] Ole found that the city no longer needed carpenters as it reeled under this financial collapse.

Nor could Ole count on getting extra work from farmers. By the end of 1892, the Dutch investment in rural lands rose beyond one million dollars. In the depression of 1893, wheat prices in the rich agricultural land of eastern Washington's Palouse plunged to a devastatingly low 30 cents a bushel, almost a two-thirds loss from earlier years. Then unseasonable rains destroyed most of the grain in the Palouse country, leaving wheat to mold and rot in the fields, which soon bankrupted farmers. Financiers foreclosed on heavily mortgaged farmland, too, and a tumble in prices left many farmers destitute, too poor to hire Ole for any building.

Eastern Washington farmers and the economy of Spokane did not experience an immediate turnaround after the Panic of 1893. Barter and trade became the currency of cash-poor farmers.[3] Hired help and local stores accepted goods, such as old saddles, produce, or livestock because no one had cash for services, groceries, dry goods, machinery, or supplies. Farmers also bought on credit, hopeful the next harvests might be good. The Estbys encountered major expenses in the early 1890s, including the cost of three doctors performing surgery on Helga and months of recovery, the $600 purchase of land, building a home, two more childbirths, plus feeding and clothing a large family. They sank into a debt cycle even before the 1893 panic. They began a pattern of borrowing a new loan to pay off the last loan.[4] This threat of slipping into destitution created intense anxiety and a sense of helplessness for Helga throughout the spring. If good fortune seemed with them earlier, providing them the means and the confidence to create their dream, the national Panic of 1893 destroyed these dreams.

With Ole's livelihood as an independent carpenter no longer in demand, the family could not depend on his earnings. Nor could he develop the farm because an injury from a horse accident left him unable to do heavy physical work.[5] Without viable income, the Estbys borrowed $1000 on the mortgage from D.K. Welt on July 6, 1894, shortly after their last daughter, Lillian, was born on March 12th. Unable to pay their mortgage or taxes during the midst of this economic depression, Helga awoke every morning haunted by the fear of foreclosure. The "unsatisfied" $1000 debt placed them in imminent danger of losing their farm.

The thought of a sheriff's sale taking all of their earthly belongings created a fear that was making Helga physically weaker. Although she was a strong woman who survived ten pregnancies, the last two pregnancies left her health more precarious. She had already undertaken risky gynecological surgery. Helga knew that a bankruptcy would tear the family apart, forcing the older sons and daughters to board out as servants or gardeners in wealthy homes. When hard times hit families, the older children often dropped out of high school to perform this menial labor. Helga longed for them to have the chances that education gave in America because she knew they were intelligent and motivated children. Those remaining with the family would probably live in a crowded dilapidated boarding house back in Spokane, placed at the mercy of unsanitary conditions and uncaring landlords. Though financially poor now, they would become poorer still if the little moments of family joy on the farm that marked their days—the hayrides and sleigh rides, grange dances, and neighborly coffees—should simply cease.

On January 18, just three days after celebrating his twelfth birthday, tragedy struck the Estby family when they lost their son Henry, possibly from heart complications with childhood rheumatoid arthritis. He was their gentle boy, who liked to help his papa saw the wood, put hay in the mangers, and cook food for the pigs. Exceptionally affectionate and loving, he unabashedly gave kisses and expressed how he missed his mama whenever she was gone.[6] Helga always had been grateful that she could help keep their children in good health, other than catching normal childhood diseases. They even avoided the diphtheria epidemic that raced through Minnesota prairie communities in the 1880s. Out of ten pregnancies, she lost only one infant after childbirth, early in their marriage.[7] She also knew how to nurse ill children back to health, so Helga was unprepared for the spiraling grief that engulfed her after losing their winsome son. This sorrow sapped her ability to sleep, to work, or even to think clearly at times.

Ole's own grief was silently borne. He carried a father's humiliating sense of inadequacy and frustration over his slow recovery from the injury that kept him from heavy labor. In late-nineteenth-century America, and especially in his Norwegian community, fathers were expected to assume responsibility in providing for their family. As a wife, Helga likely felt torn between her Norwegian sense that a wife should not refuse affection to her husband, especially when he needed comforting and reassurance, and her conviction that at thirty-six she was not ready to bear and nurse an eleventh child. Helga felt desperate and alone as she pondered a way out of their plight.

Living with the sorrow of losing her twelve-year-old son, the fear of losing the home and land she loved, and the danger of losing her emotional and physical health, Helga was thinking and praying for a solution during the spring of 1896. They had been in dire straits before—during the treacherous winter of 1880 in Minnesota—and survived. After suffering from a dangerous fall on Spokane's streets, she had sued the city, won a lawsuit, and found a female surgeon who helped restore her health. She still fervently believed that America abounded with opportunity for immigrants willing to work and take risks. Looking back at these events, she even believed that, eventually, their difficulties worked out for something good.

But a mortgage debt for a family with limited income created immense anxiety in the late 1800s. America provided no "safety net" to offer protection, nor did the immigrant Estby family have extended family nearby to turn to in times of trouble. Another Norwegian immigrant mother, who claimed a homestead in 1874 very near the Minnesota prairie land of the Estbys, described the weight of this anxiety for mothers in *Grass of the Earth: The Story of an Immigrant Family in Dakota*. As women rarely earned significant income outside of the home, the helpless anguish over an unpaid mortgage could control a life. Aargot Raaen recalled the shadow that enveloped their family life because of debt. When the family feared they could not even pay the 10% interest on their farm, Aargot (the oldest sister) brooded over the burden until she sometimes thought of nothing else. While the other children played, she would sit hidden by some low swinging bough and stare at the river; she watched the water bugs in their hopeless struggle against the swift current of the stream.

The children could not understand how the signing of a paper could change everything, but it did . . . . Moor (their mother) was very different. She went about as if she were carrying a burden. She often sat lost in thought. When alone, the children asked, "Moor, what was that paper you signed?"

"They called it a mortgage; it gives those who left the horses and the money the right to take our home unless we can pay them so much money every year for a certain number of years, besides paying the value of the horses and the money they left." A chill stole over them all. Moor and the children had barely been able to live before. How could they take over the new burden?[8]

Helga's own burning anxiety about losing the farm mirrored Moor's, but she was adamant against sitting passively by and staring at the river. The move to Mica Creek had created some of the happiest years for their large loving family, and she knew this beloved place blessed her children.

In these April days of sorrow and stress, Helga likely carried a handful of spring flowers to place beside her son's simple headstone. As she mulled over their family's threatening situation, she fought against her fears. Helga also carried within her a memory from a pivotal experience in an elementary school in Christiana (now Oslo) that gave her courage during dark times. She often shared this story with her own children. One day, when Helga was a little girl, she attended a religion class where the teacher taught the children the biblical story of "Jonah and the Whale," of how the whale swallowed Jonah and later spit him out to the sea. Her next class had been in science with a different teacher. Norway has a great seafaring tradition of whaling, and that particular day the children were studying the anatomy of whales. Helga learned that whales have small throats.

The following day Helga boldly approached the teacher in the religion class and announced that Jonah's story could not be possible because a whale's throat was not large enough to swallow a man. Troubled by little Helga's literalist response and her rejection of this biblical story, the teacher told her she should not say things like that. And then she added enthusiastically, "Don't you know, Helga, that *anything and everything* is possible with God?"[9]

Drawing on the reservoirs of strength and faith that carried her through earlier dark days, she secretly considered the riskiest opportunity she had ever been offered. Because her family believed she used this story as a kind of "life-motto," it is likely that this belief fueled her decision to attempt this trek, a trip newspapers of the era claim no other unescorted American woman had ever accomplished. A mammoth risk, but one promising her an almost unfathomable reward.

7

THE WAGER

Why do we take this trip? Well to make money . . .
I have simply got to make a stake some way,
for I don't want to lose the farm and it is the only
way I can see of saving it.

—HELGA ESTBY
SPOKESMAN-REVIEW, MAY 5, 1896

Sometime during these vulnerable months of desperation, Helga received a rare offer through "the instrumentality of a friend in the East."[1] A "wealthy woman" in New York or "eastern parties" proposed to pay Helga and her daughter Clara $10,000 if they would walk unescorted across America and meet certain stipulations of a written contract.[2] As she considered this surprising turn of events, she could hear the surging power of the Oregon Railroad and Navigation (O.R.&N.) train as it whistled by their farm, a sound of invitation coming and going to the Spokane terminal. A transcontinental train brought her own family west, and Helga began imagining walking the rails that linked the United States into one accessible continent. Sometime in April, her days of deliberation ended. Helga not only decided she could do this, but that she must. Now came the hard part, explaining to her family what she knew she wanted to do.

After the months of worry and grief, the wager must have seemed like an open door, a viable way to solve an intractable problem. She may have even believed it came as a stunning answer to her prayers for finding a way to keep their family together. Helga knew that $10,000 would not only pay the taxes and mortgage and provide survival money until Ole's health returned, but also that such abundance would assure educational opportunities for their remaining eight children. Clara and Olaf already demonstrated they could qualify to attend the new Washington State College in Pullman or the four-year private college in Spokane, and she believed the younger children seemed equally bright. What futures they could have!

The sponsoring party wanted the women to wear a type of bicycle skirt introduced at the World's Fair in Chicago in 1893 and being promoted for "the new woman" in America. The light-gray flannel costume included a short skirt that fell several inches below the knee, leggings, and a jacket.[3] Helga always dressed in the prevailing Victorian fashion that required women to wear full-length dresses or skirts that hid any "immodest" display of an ankle. These heavy petticoated garments, however, sometimes using over twelve yards of fabric, significantly confined the physical activities of women. When the bicycle craze emerged in the 1890s, the long skirts and slips hampered safe, comfortable cycling.

Fashion designers solved this with the "reform dress," but convincing American women that shorter skirts or bloomers were respectable presented a formidable challenge. Both the thought of women riding bicycles and daring such a radical change in dress met stiff resistance in some circles. The Rescue League of Washington formed to fight against women riding "the devil's agent" and wearing bicycle apparel. The organization launched a national crusade to ask clergymen and women to suppress the bicycle craze because of its vulgarity.[4] If the fashion industry, however, could use creative promotion to convince large numbers of proper women to shift their sentiments and wear the new bicycle skirts, the potential economic impact was high. Though gaining acceptance in the fashion centers of Paris and New York, few women in the rest of America wore such new fashions. The 1895 Montgomery Ward catalog, the largest mail-order business in the United States and a clothing resource for women, did not show a single shorter skirt for women to purchase.[5] Women had not forgotten the ridicule directed at earlier reformers who introduced the bloomer, a comfortable fashion that failed to be widely adopted. The sponsors could benefit from the attention Helga and Clara's audacious venture would surely generate. A reporter noted, "Mrs. Estby and daughter will be paid a certain sum of money upon their arrival in New York for their services in advertising the dress."[6]

Besides serving as a walking advertisement for fashion reform, the sponsors wanted this cross-continent achievement to prove the endurance of women.[7] As America entered the cusp of the twentieth century, progressive "new women" were challenging the common beliefs about females that often limited their choices. Biological assumptions about women's inferior physical capacities still existed, including that women were physically delicate and needed to be protected.[8] In the Victorian era, fragility in urban society women even became fashionable. "Women are too apt to regard delicacy, in its physical sense of weakness, as an essential element of beauty," noted one critical observer on women's deliberate attempts at acting frail for social prestige. "This is a false and dangerous notion, which finds expression in the affectation of paleness of complexion and tenuity of figure, which are deliberately acquired by a systematic disobedience of the laws of health."[9] Yet, physicians and advice books reinforced the prevailing belief that a woman's biology made her susceptible to disease and ill health. Physicians warned that if women made exceptional exertion, they were far more inclined to nervous exhaustion, known as neurasthenic disease, than men. The neurasthenic was "delicate and high strung, subject to fits of anxiety or even hysteria that could erupt at any time. By virtue of their anatomy, all women were susceptible and therefore had to avoid anxiety-producing and enervating situations."[10]

Physicians warned young women of Clara's age to curtail their physical and intellectual activity during their menstrual periods and gave medical advice such as, "Long walks are to be avoided . . . . also long wheel rides . . . in fact, all severe physical exertion . . . . Intense mental excitement as a fit of anger or grief or even intense joy may be injurious."[11] When Helga asked her eighteen-year-old unmarried daughter to exert herself so strenuously, this ignored society's advice that young women must guard their reproductive health. Helga's own years of hard work as a young mother on the prairie gave her confidence that doctors and society underestimated women's physical strength.

Although remnants of these beliefs permeated America, especially among the privileged classes of American women, these sentiments were being challenged by 1896. The opening of college opportunities for women also brought the development of physical education classes, partly as a way for colleges to develop women's strength and to prove that intense academic studying would not endanger their health. As the first women graduated from medical school, they began speaking to public audiences on the values of physical training. Speaking to women's clubs in the East, Dr. Mary Taylor Bissell claimed that physical exercise provided women, as well as men, with "endurance, activity and energy, presence of mind, and dexterity." She insisted that the value of physical exercise "cannot be overestimated as a sedative to emotional disturbances, and a relief from that nervous irritability and hypochondria so often engendered by a sedentary or an idle life."[12] The sponsor of the wager may have seen the positive health benefits that emerged when women, freed from constraining dress, could pursue an active physical life. Or, it simply may have been an advertising ploy to sell more reform dresses. Whichever, if two women accomplished the stunning act of walking across the mountains, plains, and deserts of America's vast continent, news of this achievement could cause a monumental shift in the public's perception of women's strength.

The "eastern parties" wrote up a formal contract with certain stipulations and a seven-month deadline that Helga agreed to and signed. Required to leave with only $5 apiece, they needed to support themselves "without begging" along the way, earning enough for food, lodging, and replacement clothes and shoes. It seems likely their required visits to political leaders in the state capitals would be interpreted as living proof of the economic capability and physical strength of ordinary women. Helga and Clara's actions could speak volumes.[13]

Helga planned to take extensive notes along the way and write a book of their adventures in hopes that the contracting parties might help sell this to the highest bidder for publication. This did not appear to be a stipulation of the sponsoring party, rather it was Helga's own attempt to increase her income.

From the beginning, they designed their monumental effort to be a public event. The first instruction from the sponsors required going to a portrait studio in Spokane for a formal photograph to send to the *New York World* newspaper. This progressive Pulitzer paper featured a weekly news column entitled "Women of the Week: Some extraordinary doings of the New Sisterhood in Unusual Fields of Feminine Effort." In the April 26, 1896 column, an announcement of the intentions of the "Two Women's Great Tramp" to walk from Spokane to New York appeared, along with a formal portrait of Helga and Clara. Noting that the women will break all records in the line of pedestrians and will travel rapidly, with very light equipment, the reporter alluded to the high-stake risks or folly of this transcontinental trek with the assessment, "They intend to write up their adventures afterwards *if they survive the experiment.*"[14]

(following pages) Helga and Clara had this photograph taken in a Spokane studio in April 1896 to send to the New York World *announcing their upcoming trip. It served as the basis for a photoengraving included in the article "Two Women's Great Tramp," which appeared in the* New York World *on April 25, 1896.*

Photograph courtesy Portch/Bahr Family Photograph Collection.
Photoengraving courtesy General Research Division,
The New York Public Library, Astor, Lenox and Tilden Foundations.
Detail of this photograph on page 82.

Two Women's Great Tramp.

MRS. H. ESTBY AND DAUGHTER, WHO WILL
WALK FROM SPOKANE TO NEW YORK.

The Spokane newspaper offices saw the startling *New York World* picture and article and published their first acknowledgment of the Estby women's trip in the May 4, 1896, issue of the *Daily Chronicle*. Entitled "Tramp to New York: An Eastern Paper Tells of Spokane Women's Plans," it told how Mrs. H. Estby and daughter are the "latest among the new women of this section of the country to attract attention in the east."[15]

For some reason, Helga gave the Spokane city address of 1725 Pacific Avenue where their children worked occasionally as domestics and gardeners, probably while attending a Spokane high school.[16] This distinctive home of the Rutter family, a leading Spokane businessman and his wife, was designed by a prestigious Northwest architect, Kirkland Cutter, and located in Spokane's wealthiest neighborhood. Because of this, the newspaper ended with a note of skepticism. "The story is an interesting one and the only fault found with it at this end of the line is that no person named Estby lives, or ever has lived at the address given nor can such a name be found in any of the city directories."[17]

To accept this wager meant Helga and Clara needed to attempt something no unescorted women before them had ever accomplished. They must undertake the hazards of crossing a continent still made up of vast stretches of wild frontier country and lofty rugged mountain passes; traverse through several Indian reservations; weather the potential ravages of blistering heat and freezing snow; walk unprotected from the threat of sudden cyclones, tornadoes, forest fires, or flash floods; resist unsavory men tempted to rob, rape, or even kill them; and survive in wilderness territory unscathed from frightened or hungry bears, mountain lions, wolves, rattlesnakes, or other wild animals. To avoid getting lost in the sparsely populated West, Helga planned to follow the railroad tracks. This meant they must negotiate long, high trestles crossing over swift rivers. And they would be wearing full-length Victorian dresses until they reached Salt Lake City.

Her husband, her Scandinavian neighbors, and her children voiced their fears and their questions. She was risking danger to herself and her daughter. How could they protect their "purity" and safety against rough men, hobos, and vagabonds who might consider women alone as easy prey? With the nation enduring harsh economic times, many unemployed men hung out along the rails to sneak rides. They could starve, unable to find food in the hundreds of miles between towns in the West, or become ill or injured while sloshing in freezing rain or snow, especially in the Rocky Mountains. Clara might be physically strong, but Helga's health clearly was more precarious after her surgery, latest childbirths, and a recent skirmish with mild consumption. Where would they find safe sleeping quarters every night, food to eat, or places to bathe, toilet, and wash their clothes when in the wilderness?

Helga heard these fears and admitted to some of her own, particularly the potential danger of being accosted by men. After entering into the contract, she considered what they needed to carry for protection. She and Clara, perhaps through a Spokane friend of the eastern sponsor, visited Spokane's Mayor Horatio Belt and requested a formal letter of introduction. He agreed to provide this document and even arranged for it to be stamped with the State Seal and the signature of the Washington State treasurer. The mayor wrote his equivalent of a calling card that asked for "kindly considerations" to Helga and Clara and affirmed that "Mrs. H. Estby has been a resident of this city and vicinity for the last nine years and is a lady of good character and reputation."[18]

On Tuesday, May 5, at 12:19, Helga and Clara, dressed "warmly but plainly," departed from the front of the *Chronicle* newspaper office at the corner of Post and Main Street to begin their arduous journey to the *New York World* newspaper office over 3000 miles away. Carrying only small bundles and a few dollars in cash, they followed the O.R.&N. railroad route for twenty-eight miles back to their home in Mica Creek. An interview covered in that afternoon's paper showed Helga's desperation and determination as she answered the question of "why they are taking this trip."

"Well, to make money," she admitted, as she described having been laid up with her own ill health for some time, and her fear they will lose their home and farm because they could not pay their taxes and mortgage. In a retort to all the doubters who urged her to reconsider because such a venture was impossible and inappropriate for women, she optimistically insisted that "they anticipate no great difficulty in making their way," and that "we have made up our minds as well as all arrangements."[19]

She mentions to one reporter, "We are just going for pleasure and to make some money," suggesting she actually looked forward to this new journey across America with her firstborn daughter, Clara. She initially appeared relaxed about the time the trip would take, expecting six months or more, and planned to be back home by Christmas. She also expressed hope that newspapers might buy articles describing their adventures along the route.

Choosing Clara to accompany her gave Helga a companion who shared her own sense of strength, intelligence, and sensitivity. As the oldest of their nine children, Clara always assumed responsibility, especially during the years when Helga's accident left her with such debilitating illness.[20] She also showed independence of thought, disagreeing with her mother on the political issues surrounding 1896. With day after day of long hours of walking ahead, Clara as a traveling partner promised interesting conversations on all that they might see. An engaging and attractive young woman, she augmented the image that mother and daughter were respectable and deserved to be treated like ladies. Being chosen by her mother did not necessarily mean she wanted to embark on this risky venture, but Clara knew Helga needed her presence.

What Helga carried inside seemed as important as the items in her satchel. Emboldened now with a decisive plan of action, she exuded a spirit of confidence, indomitable determination, and engaging intelligence, which reporters noticed. Free from the predictable daily responsibilities of birthing, nursing, and raising children that had shaped the past twenty years, Helga sounded excited about the unpredictable "pleasurable" adventures open to them as tourists when they visited major cities in America.[21]

And she carried the immigrant's mantra—to improve one's lot in life, one must be willing to journey into the unknown. During her stepfather's journey to America and her husband's move to homestead in Minnesota, she had followed them. Now Helga made her own decision on how to improve their family's life through intrepid travel. She was determined to try, despite the risks.

But this choice meant she stepped beyond traditional boundaries for women in the 1890s. Although women settling the West lived with much less rigidity to roles than eastern middle-class women, the Victorian concept of separate spheres for men and women still prevailed. Magazines, literature, and sermons elevated a woman's role in caring for her home and children, and a man's role in the public marketplace.

Motherhood, contended the editors of the popular *Godey's Lady's Book*, was the most "striking and beautiful" aspect of the "female character," providing the "fulfillment of a woman's physiological and moral destiny."[22] The widespread belief that mothers set the moral tone of a home still found expression in science, religion, and political structures of late-nineteenth-century America. "Heaven," wrote one advocate of women's elevated moral role, "has given special favors to your sex, through this simple fact or principle of dependence. It is your work to soften and refine men. Men living without you, by themselves, become savage and sinful. The purer you are, the more are they restrained, and the more are they elevated."[23]

Perhaps even more unsettling than the tangible dangers was Helga's choice to break the intangible taboo, particularly strong in Norwegian-American communities, against a mother leaving one's children. She would be leaving her eight remaining children, including Lillian, a two-year-old toddler too young to even understand why her mother left. Many believed that no proper moral woman would dare consider such a thing. Ole's best friend, Martin Siverson, clearly disapproved and could not comprehend how a mother could walk away from her family responsibilities. He expressed what others in her Norwegian community were thinking, "Women just didn't do such things!"[24]

But Helga not only held confidence in herself but also in her family. While recognizing this journey would be challenging, she believed Ole and their children could help make this work. She had returned to the Midwest for several months three years earlier in 1893, and the family proved they could sustain one another. Besides, Olaf, seventeen, Ida, fifteen, and Bertha, now fourteen, were considered old enough to work for others, so they certainly could help keep house, care for their younger brothers and sisters, and assist with the farm. Arthur, eleven, and eight-year-old Johnny could take care of the chickens and pigs and help some with four-year-old William and little Lillian. Ole's sister, Hanna, had emigrated from Norway and worked in Spokane as an ironer at the steam laundry. She could help on weekends.[25] Helga believed their kind neighbors would help in an emergency; besides, she planned to be back by Christmas. Because Ole was unable to work in carpentry until his back improved, he certainly could watch the youngest ones, Lillian and William, when school started in the fall. After all, she had managed to care for four children under age six in their one-room sod home. Ole loved the children and was a good father, and with Ida's and Bertha's help, she felt confident he could take care of them. She knew this daily care of children and the home was a rare role for a Scandinavian father, but their family life was in serious danger. Western women often entered into "men's work" to sustain a family, and she believed Ole could adapt. Maintaining proper roles provided no viable solution to their problems.

Helga acknowledged the opposition she encountered before she left Spokane. To one reporter she stated: "We were told at the start we would never make the trip, but we are confident of getting through successfully."[26] Part of her confidence came from a previous venture when she successfully walked four hundred miles alone. Although the place and reason for this earlier trek is unclear, perhaps in the Midwest to visit her family, it clearly provided an experience that infused her with a belief in their potential success.[27] To Helga, the promise of the $10,000 reward outweighed any threats of failure. She faced the question, "what does fear keep you from doing?" and decided she was unwilling to let fear or disapproval keep her from action. Feeling her family's future lay in her hands, she knew she must try to win the wager. So, with Clara at her side, Helga turned to the East.

8

UNDAUNTED BY RAIN, SLEET, AND SNOW

They conversed with enthusiasm upon their undertakings and told of the hardships, privations and snubbings which they had already submitted to with an air of perfect nonchalance. They carry revolvers which they would not hesitate to use in case of necessity.

—BEDROCK DEMOCRAT
BAKER CITY, OREGON, MAY 25, 1896

Now a quiet courage replaced Helga's earlier months of fear and anxiety. She looked forward with focused confidence, imagining one step at a time, one mile at a time, one city at a time. All they needed to do was place one foot in front of another; find food, water, and nightly shelter; stay clean; avoid violent men and wild beasts; earn funds along the way; and keep their spirits up.

The railroad routes gave them a constant guide more visible than the elusive North Star or the poorly marked maps of the sparsely populated West. Even more, the far-reaching whistles of the trains gave living proof that one could achieve the impossible.

Fabled stories abounded in America of how the men building the cross-continental railroad overcame all obstacles and naysayers. No mountain, or snowstorm, or waterway deterred the resolve of the railroad magnates and their workers from reaching their goals. Well, women could be determined, too.

Buoyant with hope, on the first day they walked twenty-eight miles along the O.R.&N. tracks from Spokane back through the spring countryside to their farm in Mica Creek for a final farewell to their family. They heard the refreshing rush and roar of the magnificent Spokane Falls and absorbed the panoramic feast of freshly plowed farmlands to hold in their memory. Early the next morning, Helga and Clara hugged and kissed the children and Ole farewell, assuring them they planned to be home for Christmas. But how does a mother explain that leaving is an act of family devotion, not desertion, especially to her toddler Lillian, or four-year-old William? Local farmers from their Little Norway community watched as the women walked away, including Martin Siverson, Ole's best friend. Helga ignored the incomprehension and stark disapproval in their eyes.[1]

For ten days they trudged south through eastern Washington, pelted by constant rains and sleet—a continuation of the worst winter in the Northwest since 1882. Chilled in their dripping wet clothes, they looked forward to arriving in the Scandinavian town of LaCrosse Junction because their map indicated this small village had a place to accommodate travelers. But, instead, they found only a depot and section house. Even more unsettling, the local Norwegians believed the women's actions scandalous, making them "undeserving vagrants." They refused to give any hospitality of shelter or food to the weary mother and daughter even though they possessed enough money to pay. So Helga and Clara took quarters in the waiting room of the depot and "fared as best we could" in their wet dresses, passing an uncomfortable night as "it was very cold."[2]

Gusty winds and rain continued to hamper their journey. After walking since 7 o'clock in the morning along the railroad, they arrived the afternoon of May 16th in Walla Walla where they wanted to rest for two days. They began their pattern of stopping by newspaper offices for free publicity when they needed to stay in a town to earn money. Helga presented their calling card that read "Mrs. H. Estby and daughter, pedestrians, Spokane to New York" at the *Walla Walla Union*. A reporter obligingly wrote a full-column article called "Are Walking for Wages" about the "plucky woman who has conceived a novel plan to raise a mortgage."[3]

Describing Helga as "a pleasant faced little woman," the article told of her attempt to save the family farm and the contract stipulation to model the "reform dress" designed by an eastern lady. Helga also described their first direct encounters with men. Rather than experiencing the predicted harassment, she stated, "We yesterday had company most of the day in the persons of two wandering gentlemen."[4] The women's spirit of tourism and adventure emerged, or at least their desire to gather interesting stories along the way. They mentioned their intention to visit the Cripple Creek mining district in Colorado, all the large cities along the way, and "everything of interest." Helga even wanted to visit the Washington State penitentiary and garrison before leaving for Pendleton. Walla Walla was also the site of the Whitman mission, where Cayuse Indians, realizing the missionaries and settlers brought the measles epidemic that decimated their tribe, killed Marcus and Narcissa Whitman thirty-eight years earlier in 1848. Narcissa also broke new ground as the first Anglo-American woman to cross the continent on a Conestoga wagon with her husband in 1837.

Before Helga and Clara reached Pendleton, they received a "good fortune" ride from a Mr. Mason who was traveling in his own wagon from Sprague, Washington, to Pendleton. Saying this wagon ride was "the first ride they have had since leaving home," they clarified the contract stipulations on transportation to a reporter, saying they must walk on foot, or go by vehicle other than a railroad vehicle "in which they may be invited, without remuneration, to take a ride."[5]

From Pendleton they followed the Union Pacific track through the Umatilla Indian Reservation, land of around one thousand members of the Walla Walla, Cayuse, and Umatilla Tribes.[6] The railway ran

Helga and Clara crossed through the Umatilla Reservation of the Confederated Tribes of the Cayuse, Umatilla, Nez Perce, and Walla Walla along the Umatilla River near Pendleton, Oregon.

through the reservation along the silver thread of the Umatilla River, banked by cottonwood and hawthorn trees and steep bluffs. Walking the rails took the women directly through the land where Indians set up their encampments along the riverbanks.

Then they started the climb up the Blue Mountains, an eastern Oregon mountain range of great scenic beauty. But these were the same mountains that earlier proved so challenging for travelers, oxen, and wagons on the Oregon Trail. At over 4100 feet, this rugged mountain pass tested the women's physical endurance. Beautiful in summer, the snows were only partially melted by May. Often the previous day's thaw froze into ice during the overnight frost, adding to challenging drifts, snow banks, and sheets of ice on the steep climb and descent of this 45-mile trek over the mountains. Even in a milder spring, locals encouraged crossing in late summer. They believed that "no sane man who values his life and health should attempt the journey before April or May," but Helga and Clara needed to try now.[7] Where the snow had recently melted, the mud, mire, and high water created additional dangers as they forged across streams several times a day in their long skirts. They did not carry blankets, boots, or a change of clothes, so they risked hypothermia from the steep drop in temperatures at night, when temperatures rarely rose above zero. They finished the long dreary descent down Devil's Pinch, hungry, wet, and exhausted, undoubtedly delighted to see the beautiful Grande Ronde Valley. Yet, after their first treacherous mountain crossing, they had proved to themselves they possessed exceptional fortitude and strength.

On the way down the mountain before reaching La Grande, Oregon, a tramp followed and threatened them for several days. "At a lonely point [he] attempted to intercept" them. They protested and tried to avoid him. But he persisted. Frightened by his actions, when he "refused to desist" and instead attacked, Helga shot a bullet through this "dudishly looking fellow's leg." Shaken by this face-off with a dangerous man and her need for lethal action, she was "pleased to announce that they were not arrested for this."[8] This first incident defending themselves gave Helga growing confidence that she possessed the mettle to protect them, if necessary. The town of La Grande, situated at the foot of the Blue Mountains, was a welcome relief. A farming community in a long fertile valley, surrounded by mountains abundant with fir, pine, and tamarack trees, it promised a place for food and rest.

Then, by the afternoon of May 24, they arrived at the *Bedrock Democrat* newspaper office in Baker City, Oregon. The reporter described the revolver-toting women as weather beaten and sun brown, and Clara as "tall, well built, rather pleasant appearing, and of mature years." Helga expressed hope that they might earn part of their travel funds by "furnishing reports to New York and San Francisco newspapers." She recognized that working in towns absorbed valuable time from their seven-month deadline, more time than she originally imagined. They planned to continue selling portraits of themselves, which was a quicker way to gain funds. She said, however, "if driven to extremes," they will accept any employment that may be offered them at cities through which they may pass.[9]

The enthusiasm of the women caught the reporter's attention, even as they casually told of the hardships they had encountered already. Getting healthier each day, Helga noted that she doubted she would need the medicine she carried in her knapsack as "the exposure has improved her indifferent health and given both herself and daughter appetites like bears."[10]

Helga and Clara stopped at Boise's Idaho Daily Statesman *newspaper to get publicity about their trip. They stayed a week working to replenish funds needed for food, lodging, and clothes.*

For the first time, she admitted how much her husband's inability to provide for the family motivated her decision, something she never said quite so publicly in Spokane. When questioned as to their motives in undertaking the trek, Helga said that it had been first conceived through "the inability of her husband to maintain the family." This fueled her determination "to do something herself" to help retrieve some of their lost belongings. If they succeeded, it would help her to recover the farm which is "all but hypothecated."11

So many people expressed concerns over the danger of unsavory men that when Helga and Clara began, they admitted to harboring some of these fears too, especially potential assaults by isolated ranchers and cowboys, hobos, and highwaymen. But by the time they arrived in Baker City, their fears began dissolving. Their many kind encounters with others gave Helga and Clara a growing confidence in people they met and in their own capacity to cope. Farmers and townspeople must have offered them shelter because they stayed only one more shivering night in a cold outbuilding before reaching Baker City. The reporter noted, "The courtesy shown up to the present time, with very few exceptions, has caused the dread to almost entirely disappear. They say they are now afraid of nothing and will either conquer or perish in the attempt to succeed."[12]

They continued south and east, eventually crossing the Snake River. They could not have foreseen that this May would have the heaviest rainfall in thirty-three years in the Boise region, which caused the rivers to rise precipitously. Coming from Emmet, the deep waters forced them to cross the river and walk the railroad tracks before they entered the city on June 4. They arrived to a city in alarm over the raging Boise river, which had risen six inches in forty-eight hours. A "force of men" had worked feverishly to retrieve giant logs that had escaped from a boom and shattered bridge pilings in the furious waters. Citizens also built levees to contain the flood waters threatening to cut off South Boise and the city.[13]

During these first thirty days they had successfully traversed through their first mountain range, waded through swollen river waters, and trudged through spring snows until arriving safely to Boise, Idaho. Only three days of nice weather occurred in that month; nevertheless, they established a rhythm averaging twenty-seven miles a day and proved they possessed the will to protect themselves when necessary. In need of rest and money to continue, they stopped at the newspaper office and presented their card.

In the June 5 *Idaho Daily Statesman*, Helga told the reporter that the parties putting up the wager did not care to have their names divulged until the women reached their destination. Impressed with their physical energy and positive spirits in spite of the obstacles they encountered, the reporter observed, "The women did not seem to be discouraged and stated they hoped to return to Spokane by Christmas."[14]

Helga and Clara raised funds in Boise by cooking, cleaning, selling pictures, "anything but chopping wood." They also entered Boise during a week when the press avidly covered discussions over women's suffrage. Three days before Helga arrived, a large gathering came to city hall to hear an equal suffrage talk by Mrs. Laura Jones, which the *Idaho Statesman* reporter believed was "a convincing presentation of the reasons why women should be given the ballot. It was intensely logical throughout, relieved by anecdotes and humor sufficiently to keep the audience in a constant good humor."[15] Boise's active equal suffrage club was also praised that week in the press.

Before they left Boise, Helga and Clara began their own engagement with America's political leadership by calling on Governor W. J. McConnell of Idaho. He added his signature to the document of introduction from Mayor Belt and included a kind personal note, "He is acquainted with Mayor Belt and vouches for the integrity of the bearers."[16] They left the streets of Boise with their finances shored up, their supplies fortified, and with eagerness to continue their journey.

9 Hot, Hungry, and Hopeful

"Thus far," said Mrs. Estby, "we have had a pretty hard time . . . I assure you when the trip is over we will never undertake such a trip again."

—DESERET NEWS
SALT LAKE CITY, JULY 8, 1896

A few days after leaving Boise, Helga and Clara took the grievous shortcut that led to their stark days lost in the Snake River lava beds. They followed the Union Pacific rails down to Gooding and cut east to Shoshone where they arrived on June 26. They evidently then tried correcting this by leaving the rails and crossing over the Snake River Plain. Clearly unprepared for this mistake, they wandered around the molten maze of lava for three days "without a mouthful to eat."[1] While growing hunger drained their energy, they also needed to stay alert for rattlesnakes hidden among the charcoal rocks. On the third night, a headlight from a distant Union Pacific train shone in the night and provided a beacon to direct their way back to the rails.[2]

After this near catastrophe, they continued south to Utah, committed now to staying with their original plan to follow the rails. The sparsely populated land in southern Idaho provided no alternative but to walk through miles and miles of hot, dry, lonely territory, with no towns, railroad stations, or even farms to find meals or shelter. It was not unusual for them to find only one meal a day and they felt fortunate when they ate twice a day. The barrenness of Utah, generally bereft of foliage except here and there in narrow, rock-ribbed gorges, seemed inhospitable after living in the lush land of the Pacific Northwest. By now, electric storms, flash floods, rain, and snow had slowed their walk, caused detours, and changed Helga's almost cavalier confidence that crossing this vast American continent on foot might be easy. In classic understatement, she describes these dangers and difficulties to a reporter, "We had considerable trouble in making our way through Idaho and over the mountains."[3]

Entering northern Utah, which had just received statehood in 1896, Helga and Clara saw the land chosen and settled by members of the Church of Jesus Christ of Latter-day Saints in their great migration for religious freedom in the 1840s and 50s. Coming into Brigham City, Helga gained a sense of the magnitude of Mormon influence in this region when she saw her first tabernacle rising high above this small town located about forty-five miles north of Salt Lake City. After tromping for days in arid land and bleak isolation, Helga and Clara marveled at how the hardworking citizens irrigated the desert and built a town with schools, churches, businesses, and sycamore-lined streets.

Knowing of hostilities between Native Americans and white settlers during the westward expansion made Helga nervous when they first encountered Indians. One day, while Clara and Helga walked through Utah, a band of young Indians spotted the women and stopped them. One spoke a little English and directed them to empty their satchels on the ground. After looking over Helga and Clara's skimpy supplies of sketchpads, pencils, lanterns, revolvers, and medicine, he seemed puzzled by the women's curling iron. He signaled he wanted to see what it was used for, so Clara demonstrated how she curled her silky brown hair into ringlets. He seemed satisfied, returned all their items, and left the relieved women to continue on their journey.[4]

These late June days also brought Helga and Clara near the Great Salt Lake and wetlands, one of America's prime resting places for waterfowl. Surrounded by salt flats and sage plains, hundreds of thousands of migratory birds nest there in the spring. During the month of Helga and Clara's arrival, the white-faced ibis, Canada geese, great blue herons, snowy egrets, white pelicans, shorebirds, cormorants, and dozens of other species made this their home. They likely saw the thousands of colony-nesting California gulls—the common white, black, and gray gulls that are legendary in Mormon history for rescuing the settlers' crops in 1848 from an infestation of crickets.[5]

The blistering July heat forced them to begin walking at night, and they arrived in Salt Lake City at 8 o'clock in the morning on July 8. They stopped by the *Deseret News* because they intended to remain for a week or so to rest up and work to "get a few pennies to help us further along." They also admitted to their first discouragement, describing the trouble making their way through Idaho and over the mountains.

"Thus far," said Mrs. Estby to the local reporter, "we have had a pretty hard time. The journey, however, is not what it is cracked up to be and I can assure you that when the trip is over I will never undertake such a trip again." But then her confidence returned with her hope that "it has to get much better now" as the districts through which they will pass are more thickly settled than those which they have already traversed.[6]

After the previous days of desolation, Salt Lake City renewed Helga's spirits like a refreshing oasis. With a population of over 100,000, Salt Lake City was the pride of Utah settlers because of its vital commerce, arts, and industries, and as the pilgrimage destination for their faith. Helga and Clara planned to tour many of the points of interest and looked forward to visiting temple square and the stunning elliptical sandstone tabernacle with its bolted latticework and dome-shaped roof.[7] Designed for exceptional acoustics, the

The women visited W.W. Wells, the governor of Utah, on July 11, and saw the Mormon Tabernacle in Salt Lake City.

Courtesy Denver Public Library, Western Historical Collection, photo by H.S. Poley, P378.
Detail of this photograph on page 112.

tabernacle drew local citizens and visitors alike to hear the beauty of the choir's performances.

Mormons, who considered themselves on a mission from God, founded Salt Lake City in 1847 to establish a religious utopia in the wilderness, a model city where they could practice, without persecution, their vision of a close-knit communitarian society. However, with the completion of the transcontinental railroad in 1869 and the development of mining and smelting, their geographic isolation ended. By 1890, the flood of immigrants created diversity with more than fifty percent of the population non-Mormon. Helga and Clara entered a deeply divided city, where Mormons and non-Mormons usually lived in separate residential neighborhoods, attended separate schools, joined separate fraternal and commercial organizations, and battled over social and cultural issues.[8]

By 1896, the changing city resembled other western cities undergoing rapid urbanization. Similar attitudes toward the "necessity" of prostitution that existed in Spokane allowed prostitution to be tolerated in Salt Lake City, which housed a thriving "red-light" district in the heart of downtown. Legal businesses, such as cigar and liquor stores, lined Commercial Street with "female boarders" in the upstairs of the houses. An urban working-class ghetto emerged west of the railroad tracks. With the extraction of copper, lead, silver, and gold in Utah, five smelting companies caused significant pollution to drift into Salt Lake City through a smoke belt between Murray and the city. But the city had cleaned up another pollution problem in 1890 when a major sanitation effort led to the installation of five miles of sewer pipe in the downtown area, eliminating the fetid sources of earlier epidemics.

Now well-dressed women passed to and from the shops along Temple Street. Through an elaborate canal system, the Mormons transformed the parched land until the city teemed with beautiful flower gardens, backyard orchards, and parks. A well-planned city that some called the Paris of Utah, Salt Lake City presented spacious avenues with beautiful hotels, markets, libraries, and even a museum.

While in Utah, they managed to arrange a visit to the office of Governor Wells and he added his signature to their document from Mayor Belt. He clearly treated the women with respect and welcome as they reported to the *Deseret News* that Utah had a "very excellent chief executive."[9] The *Deseret News* reporter described Helga and Clara as intelligent women who "converse freely and fluently," were clad in fairly good apparel, and were taking notes on the way because they expected to write a book at the completion of their journey. Recognizing their stunning achievement so far, the reporter noted that "the only other woman known to have attempted a similar feat left from San Francisco with two men and dogs; when she arrived at Salt Lake City she quickly boarded a train to return home."[10]

In Salt Lake City they donned the bicycle skirts that the original contract stipulated they model. For some, perhaps even the sponsor of the wager, the emancipation of women from conventional and deforming fashions became linked with women's growing freedom in society. "Until woman is allowed to have ankles, there is no hope for her brains," claimed one advocate for the reform dress.[11] By 1896, "women's leg freedom" had become a hotly contested argument. As the *Chicago Tribune* stated, "No sane person can possibly dispute the truth that women have just as much right to leg freedom as men. For some inscrutable reason this liberty has been denied them."[12] For fashion designers, popularizing a viable new mode of dressing with knickerbockers or a shorter skirt promised enormous economic gain.

But breaking through the cultural taboos presented a major challenge. Progressive women, wanting lightness, comfort, and ease of motion joined the "rational dress movement" and formed a society that protested against tightly fitted corsets and heavily weighted skirts. Such extravagant fashions rendered healthy exercise almost impossible, but even more important, clearly affected women's health. As women doctors began practicing medicine, they recognized all the unhealthy effects of irrational fashions and were especially convinced that corsets could cause a displaced or prolapsed uterus, atrophy of abdominal muscles, damage to the liver, displacement of the stomach and intestines, and constriction of the chest and ribs.[13]

In eastern circles, especially among educated females, women's clubs began to challenge cultural fashions and linked this to the health of women. At the Brooklyn Health Culture Club, a female physician elaborated on the implications of wearing dresses that touch the ground. "It jars her back violently, hurts her head and tells on her nerves." She explained how every inch on the bottom of a skirt counted in weight and fatigue and affected a woman's ability to digest food when their stomachs were so pinched and pressed with bands. "Is it any wonder that we have congestions, tumors and all sorts of things?"[14] A teacher of physical culture for women modeled the "short" skirt that she stated was all the rage in Paris; the "rule" was to wear a skirt between five and eight inches from the ground. From reporter's descriptions, this fits the type of skirts that the sponsor asked Helga and Clara to wear.

Of equal concern was the filth that long skirts picked up from the streets and brought into the home, and the drag upon spine, hips, and abdomen that caused a state of exhaustion. "More women die annually in our country from the effects of faulty dressing than from all contagious diseases combined and the invalids from this cause alone form a great host that no man can number," insisted Dr. Emily Bruce.[15] Yet, a female doctor in 1896 who tried to convince women to discard corsets and wear more sensible dress complained, "In nine cases out of ten a woman clings to her corset as the drowning man clings to a straw."[16]

Such radical ideas challenging cultural norms caused the then President of the United States, Grover Cleveland, to distrust and denounce the popular women's club movement that sometimes fostered these discussions. "These [women's clubs] are harmful in a way that directly menaces the integrity of our homes and the benign disposition and character of our women's wifehood and motherhood," the President insisted. "I believe that it should be boldly declared that the best and safest club for a woman to patronize is her home."[17]

When Helga and Clara changed into this costume, their apparel attracted immediate attention, and reporters almost always commented on their shorter skirts. Now perceived by the public as "new women," it is possible they began to perceive themselves differently, too. While dressed in their long Victorian skirts, they presented a certain conventional and safe respectability to the farmers, ranchers, and small-town people they relied on to provide them with hospitality. These more practical clothes, required by the stipulation of their contract, gave them a new leg freedom as they forged streams, climbed mountains, and walked over twenty-five miles each day. But now, before any one even talked with them, their reform costumes inevitably caused a stir, perhaps even suspicion.

They started wearing shorter skirts in Salt Lake City as part of their contract, a new experience for Helga and Clara.

Courtesy Portch/Bahr Family Photograph Collection

C. S. Ricker,

1313 Wash. Ave. S. Minneapolis,

10
NIGHT TERRORS

They lit a huge bonfire at night for protection, but
stayed awake with guns in hand.

—LEBANON EVENING NEWS,
DECEMBER 19, 1896

Staying focused steadily on their goal, they headed northeast from Salt Lake City to Wyoming, stopping on the way in Park City, Utah, to visit the silver mines. Perhaps emboldened by their new leg freedom and Helga's strong curiosity, they claim "they went 1500 feet underground to observe"—clearly unusual actions for women.[1] From there they traversed through the Heber Valley along the Union Pacific rails through the Wasatch Mountains, across wetland meadows into Silver Creek Canyon. Here they described climbing halfway down the canyon whose sides descended three hundred feet almost perpendicularly. "We managed to get part way down," said Helga to a reporter, "but had to return after nearly losing our lives."[2]

They entered Wyoming through Evanston at a time when violent clashes in northern Wyoming among big ranchers, rustlers, and settlers in the Johnson County War in 1892, and the murder of Chinese mineworkers in the Rock Springs Massacre in 1887 had given the new state a reputation of vigilante lawlessness. Sparsely populated, far more men than women lived here. But it was not just romanticized cowboys on the ranges. Miners were needed to extract the coal, and workers toiled for the railroads. Mine owners and railroad captains recruited cheap laborers from around the world, including Mexico, England, Ireland, Scotland, Denmark, Finland, and China. A climate of racial tension pervaded the workforce, and outbreaks of violence persisted.

Helga and Clara needed to walk more than 350 miles to Cheyenne, first crossing an area known as the Red Desert, a dry land receiving less than ten inches of rain a year. This sagebrush land fed some of the world's largest herds of pronghorn antelope, thousands of head of sheep, plus cougars and grizzlies. With long distances between towns, they again faced problems finding food and shelter, and spent hours and hours of tedious trudging in the vast great basin. For three days and nights they walked without food and slept in the open air.[3] The scorching heat in August, coupled with bouts of hunger, made reaching their twenty-seven-mile goal each day a grueling challenge.

While in the wilderness, their terror of mountain lions often kept them awake, especially when they heard them prowling nearby. In Wyoming they had a

Helga and Clara needed to cross the Union Pacific's highest bridge, the Dale Creek trestle near Laramie, Wyoming. The bridge was an engineering marvel at 150 feet above the creek, but terrifying to walk across.

Courtesy Colorado Historical Society, photo by Wm. H. Jackson, CHS-11046, 20101046.

narrow escape from a gray mountain lion "as big as a man" that followed them for twelve miles. "Being acquainted with the animal's traits, we knew they never attacked from behind and never except by running and springing upon a victim," explained Helga to a reporter. "We kept up a steady pace and kept the animal about ten feet behind us." They lit a huge fire at night for protection but stayed awake with guns in hand.[4]

Most of the time they spent the nights in Union Pacific section houses along the railroad tracks, and sometimes farmers and ranchers invited them into their homes. When Helga and Clara traveled through Rock Springs, they found tangible evidence of the

Many nights Helga and Clara slept in railroad depots, such as this one in Rock River, Wyoming. The depots were often the only shelter across long, desolate stretches of the West.

Courtesy Union Pacific Historical Collection.
Detail of this photograph on page 124.

racial tensions among coal-mine workers when they saw armed federal troops in the city. Ever since the powerful Union Pacific Railroad hired low-paid Chinese laborers in 1875, tensions flared between the union miners who sought better wages and working conditions and the foreigners they resented for taking their jobs. When a strike situation arose again in 1885, a labor riot erupted and a white mob torched Chinatown, a section of Rock Springs. They killed at least twenty-eight Chinese miners, forcing miners to flee into the desert hills where more died of exposure. Federal troops, called in by the governor, stayed in town for thirteen more years to protect the interests of the Union Pacific and the lives of the Chinese miners.[5]

Walking through the Sweetwater region of Wyoming, they passed through Carbon, where the Union Pacific opened up seven coal mines in the traditional lands of the Cheyenne and Arapaho Indians. Helga felt the pain of her son's death again when she saw the tiny gravesites of the town's children. Many died from cholera from an imported, contaminated water supply in the early years of mining.[6] On their way to Rawlins, they saw more cattle than people in the vast stretches of dry land in the flat plains of the Great Divide Basin. The sounds of songbirds broke the long stretches of solitude.

After Rawlins, they began the climb through the Medicine Bow region. Constant blowing winds that raced through the channel between the Hanna Basin uplift and Elk Mountain dusted their clothes and skin with grit and gravel. By the time they reached Laramie on August 26, they clearly felt they had accomplished another milestone. The *Daily Sun Leader* described the wager, the threatening moments, and the women's persistent optimism even though they now had slept out eight nights and sometimes had to go without food. "They had been lost in forests, had adventures with mountain lions, but still they trudged on in their short gray suits and came up smiling."[7]

As news of their unusual venture became known among the railroad men, some began to leave bottles of water along the tracks to quench the women's thirst in the blistering heat. As working-class men who endured the depression of 1893, they understood the vulnerability of a family losing a home. This unexpected "kindly consideration" gave Helga and Clara firsthand experience in the ways men in Wyoming showed respect toward women.[8] This respect extended far beyond acts of kindness and courtesy. Since 1869, the Territory of Wyoming had given women the right to vote, and when Wyoming entered the union in 1890 as the forty-fourth state, it became the first with women's suffrage. Women served on juries and held public office. As a conventional mother deeply immersed in the daily demands of caring for nine children, nothing indicated that Helga held much interest in politics before this extensive journey through America. But sometime during the walk, her interest in politics awakened, perhaps from earlier memories of the suffrage movement in Manistee during her childhood. It is possible that here in Wyoming, known as the Equality State, Helga began to wonder, "Should such rights be given to Washington women too?"

Crossing over the Laramie Mountains, summer storms and flash floods washed away bridges, which caused significant delays in their travel. After one bridge washout, they walked six miles through water

two feet deep before they could climb up on the oppo-
site bank of the river.[9] In eastern Wyoming, Helga
and Clara entered the fabled land of the cattle drives,
where wealthy Texas ranchers fattened their cattle on
the thick carpet of tall prairie grasses on an open
range. Needing to protect their landholdings, small-
scale ranchers began to fence in their land from graz-
ing, which infuriated the cattle barons. Helga and
Clara heard stories of the serious clashes, strife, and
murders in the region from the local ranchers or
farmers with whom they stayed.

But during August, excitement stirred around
another topic of conversation at the dinner tables and
in the towns of southern Wyoming as citizens looked to
America's future in the 1896 presidential election. The
dynamic young Democratic candidate from Nebraska,
William Jennings Bryan, surprised the Republicans
with his magnetic grassroots campaign. The nation still
reeled from the sustained financial depression of the
early 1890s. Bankruptcies had caused thousands of
industries to shut down and left over twenty percent of
men unemployed.[10] Many rode the Union Pacific rails
into Wyoming looking for work.

Hard times devastated farmers, too, who often
sank into debt with heavy mortgages, just like the
Estby family. Even when farmers produced abundant
crops, high interest rates charged by banks and exor-
bitant shipping costs charged by the railroads ate
their profits. This fueled their growing distrust of

concentrated wealth, corporate greed, and big business monopolies and trusts. In an increasingly urbanized and industrialized America, ailing farmers felt forgotten, and many joined the Populist party to fight for reform of the injustices they experienced. In rousing language, Bryan built his campaign to tap into the needs of those he called the "struggling masses" and "humbler members of society." He reaffirmed their worth to the country, citing them as the Americans who produced the crops and goods that allowed the nation to live.

He also excoriated the "capitalistic class" that "owns money, trades in money and grows rich as the people grow poor."[11] Bryan named and identified their fears of abuse from the powerful corporate elite, from Wall Street, and from the railroad and mining magnates. Captains of industry such as John D. Rockefeller (Standard Oil), J.P. Morgan (banking financier), and James J. Hill (Union Pacific) passionately supported William McKinley and the Republican agenda, and they wielded enormous political clout. Bryan fought openly against "the heads of these great trusts" that he believed put corporate profit above people.[12] Poor farmers and workers, especially in the West and South, flocked to hear him speak as he stumped as the "champion of the people." Some supporters even infused him with religious symbolism, calling him the "new Christ of Humanity" who had "come to loose the chains of plutocracy from the people." Whether voters saw him as a "mouthing slobbering demagogue" or the savior of the common man, his campaign galvanized interest in the election.[13]

Helga read newspaper accounts of the mesmerizing young orator and saw the hope he ignited in ordinary folk like herself, even while arousing enormous disdain of many powerful business, clergy, and political leaders. One conservative Republican called him "the blatant wild ass of the prairie," and others feared his demagogic, divisive appeal.[14] Helga began to form her own opinion of Bryan. She knew intimately the fear of financial ruin and the callous power of the financial elite who threatened to foreclose and take their family's home away. Both in Spokane, and now across America, she saw firsthand the growing gap between the extremely wealthy families and the desperately destitute families. Visual reminders existed in almost every town and city within the elegant mansions and enormous ranches of the rich, and the squalid shacks and hovels of the dirt-poor. Walking the rails, she knew "on the other side of the tracks" often meant a literal dividing line in a town, keeping people of different social and economic classes apart as effectively as a moat around a medieval castle. She began to notice another division in America, the racial and ethnic separations, which she had paid scant attention to when surrounded by the Scandinavian community.

Each step she took across America represented her own defiant and last-ditch effort to prevent this destitution to befall her family. The enormity of her risk was linked in direct proportion to the enormity of her fear. It was also a highly personal act. But in Bryan's vision, and some of the populists he represented, Helga heard a collective effort to reform America. He urged the farmers, laborers, and small businessmen of the country to unite in opposition to the concentrated and arrogant wealth of giant corporations and monopolists. Bryan's was a fervent crusade for the unlimited coinage of "free silver" and a bimetallic money system to restore the country's economic health. After Congress closed down the coinage of silver in 1873, the nation used only the gold standard. Bryan argued that this caused a shortage of money that most hurt the poorest classes in America. To restore the depressed economy, he advocated to allow the coinage of both silver and gold, a return to bimetallism, which would stimulate silver production and put more money in circulation. Helga agreed. Important silver mines in Coeur d'Alene and Wallace, Idaho, just east of Spokane Falls, impacted Helga's hometown economy, perhaps shaping her sympathies toward this position.

Helga knew Major William McKinley, the Republican candidate for the presidency, believed just as ardently that only the gold standard guaranteed a sound money system. Besides, Clara favored him.[15] With time on her hands now to think, and the fervor of debate over the 1896 election alive in every town,

Helga pondered political solutions to the troubles permeating the country. Rooted with a pioneer's pride that she and Ole held their fate in their own hands, yet troubled by the turbulent setbacks of the past years, Helga wondered if Bryan's call for more government curbs on the abusive power of corporations might help in situations like hers. It sounded logical to her when he argued that the government that does not restrain the strongest citizen from injuring the weakest citizen fails to do its duty. During hours of walking, she had a chance to hear why Clara felt differently. Ardent conversations enlivened the monotony of their days.

By the time they reached the Wyoming capital of Cheyenne, their physical stamina and mental toughness had been tested for 350 harsh and lonesome miles across Wyoming. Their challenges came from nature, from wild animals, from the relentless barren distances. But they never mentioned any difficulty with lawless men; in fact, they spoke more of the good treatment and respect they received. In Helga's experience, the state that gave legal representation and respect to women extended that to personal respect. What other surprises remained ahead?

11 "NEW WOMEN'S" ACTIONS AND OLD VICTORIAN ATTITUDES

*The Mexican cattle and rattle snakes made life a
terror for them in Eastern Colorado .... They are
certainly a strong testimony of woman's endurance
and ability to care for herself.*

—PLYMOUTH (INDIANA) REPUBLIC
NOVEMBER 19, 1896

An unseasonable cooling trend, causing
daytime temperatures to dip fifteen degrees below
normal to the low 50s, provided cloudy days for comfortable walking from Cheyenne to Denver. The cin-
derblock rails, however, tore the soles on their shoes,
so on September 1, they stopped in Greeley, Colorado,
at the King Shoe Company to buy some new "stout
footwear."[1] A reporter heard about the "two females
that stalked" into Greeley from "parts unknown." The
$10,000 wager and their "claim" to have been "hoof-
ing" it from Spokane, with the goal of continuing to
New York, seemed unfathomable. The reporter con-
ceded, however, "that they were doing the pedestrian
stomp, no one could dispute," for their "appearance
indicated wear and tear." They were "tanned like

baseball players and wore a faded, frayed-out Weary Waggles cut bias." The reporter concluded skeptically, "They gave their names as Mrs. H. Estby and daughter Clara. The fakes left this city for Denver."[2]

Such doubts over a woman's claim to have walked unscathed through five sparsely populated western states, across high mountain passes and nearly deserted deserts did not surprise Helga. Her family and neighbors in Mica Creek doubted her, too. So, Helga kept a detailed notebook, recording faithfully the events and observances of the day "for a book which they calculated to publish when they got through."[3] She also sent hundreds of pages home to Ole and their children, keeping them aware of their daily progress.[4] She likely included the little things that reporters seldom asked her about, like how the carol of the meadowlarks gave joy to their morning walks or how she and Clara rubbed each other's feet at night to ease the pain. Did they include details on bathing in mountain streams, or did their modesty or fears of molestation keep them from such exposure? She surely wrote about the Indian Chief who befriended them and gave them trinkets that she proudly wore and how her earlier fear of Indians was changing.[5]

Besides the important connection with the family she loved, she believed their experiences would intrigue others. She wanted readers to hear about the generous hotel owners who gave them housing and refused to accept payment, and of the many farmhouse families who kindly sheltered and fed them. An accomplished seam-

While in Denver, the vibrant capital of Colorado, Helga visited Governor Albert W. McIntire's office and added his prestigious signature to her document.

stress, interested in fabric and design, she noticed the homemade quilts, lacework, and stylish fashions she saw in farmhouses and cities. These were good stories, of a good land and good people. Her abiding love for America, nurtured as an immigrant child, deepened daily.

Now much more interested in politics and society, her letters home likely told of her thoughts about women having the right to vote, what westerners said about Bryan, or the response of strangers to their

The "pedestrians" exerted exceptional effort to visit Cripple Creek, which like Leadville, Colorado, had labor unrest in the mining district that kept federal troops in the region.

Courtesy Colorado Historical Society,
photo by O'Keefe and Stockdorf, CHS-X4591, 20004591.

short skirts. Did she admit to her discouragement, or did she abide by the western code of "swallowing your complaints...don't talk about trouble"?[6] Each day of travel expanded Helga's awareness of her own physical and mental strength. But it also immersed her into the swirling ideas of a turn-of-the-century country in tension and transition.

Outside of Denver, a bold highwayman attempted to rob them. Undaunted, Clara sprayed the dangerous man with her pepper gun and "rolled him down a hill."[7] This could be the same robber of whom Helga later claimed proudly, "I knocked him down."[8] They arrived unharmed to Denver, the capital of Colorado, a vibrant city of over 100,000 residents that emerged as a regional center for mining, transportation, and commercial interests as settlers moved west.

In Denver, Helga saw women's strong interest in the campaign for the presidency because this election gave them their first chance to cast their ballot. Colorado passed women's suffrage three years earlier in 1893, and now women actively organized for both McKinley and Bryan. In 1877, an earlier suffrage referendum for Colorado failed, partly out of many women's apathy or disdain for the reform.[9] But this changed in the following years, accelerated through the formation and growth of less threatening women's organizations, such as the Women's Christian Temperance Union, Ladies' Aid Societies, literary clubs, and unions. Women in Colorado began to have a variety of opportunities for participation in social issues, intellectual stimulation, and political organization, and the idea of suffrage stayed alive. With an active Women's Temperance Union, middle-class women began to see the ballot as a powerful tool for moral reform. The women Helga and Clara met throughout both Wyoming and Colorado in 1896 held a political power that Helga and Clara now recognized they lacked. While in Denver, Helga visited another powerful politician, Governor Albert W. McIntire, who added his signature to her document.

Helga wanted to visit the Cripple Creek gold-mining area where labor troubles were brewing, even though this detour added a few extra days, and even though two raging fires in April had destroyed the business district and hundreds of homes. So, on Sunday, September 6, they followed the railroad spur into the mountains. With the economic depression following 1893, miners throughout America were upset both by loss of jobs and unjust salaries. The miners in Cripple Creek, by striking, prevented the lengthening of the working day in 1893, and their union won another substantial victory after striking against mine owners in 1894.[10] Because Ole belonged to a union, and Spokane Falls served the nearby mining areas, Helga may have been interested in labor unrest, or she may have been gathering observations for her potential book.

Helga's frustration at their slow pace surfaced. The sponsor's twin stipulations that the women must earn their own way across and meet a time deadline placed them in a double bind. With the journey only half completed and just over two months of time remaining, being bound by their contract to "not receive a cent in aid of their own expenses" was proving unworkable.[11] The pattern of staying in a town for a few days to earn their own way by washing, scrubbing, or cleaning houses simply took too long.

Somewhere in Colorado, Clara fell on rocks. She severely sprained her ankle, which caused a ten-day delay and further risked their ability to fulfill the contract.[12] With the December deadline looming, they needed to find a faster way to earn their travel expenses. Time was getting short.

Helga and Clara saw an abundance of natural beauty in the American landscape, such as the front range of the Rocky Mountains at Pikes Peak near Colorado Springs.

Their trek out of Colorado Springs took them past the splendor of Pikes Peak, where the early morning sun cast a purple hue over the imposing mountain. Returning to Denver, they cut through the northeast part of Colorado, following the rails to Omaha.

As the ordinary and the famous citizens of America began to learn about the Estby women's achievement, the sheer audacity of their accomplishment disputed the validity of the commonly held beliefs that women were physically inferior to men, they were a weaker sex that must be protected, and that biology was destiny. Victorian restraints emphasized that the female body should always be covered, that ladies must never sweat, and that physical exertion should take place in private. When women pedaled or walked the streets without corsets or padded clothing, and shortened their skirts, they broke with genteel conventions.

In the mid-1870s, a few women challenged these assumptions when they competed as pedestrian endurance walkers in women's footraces, performing before large crowds in America's major cities. Two such female athletes, American Mary Marshall and German Bertha von Hillern vied against each other in six-day walking races in Chicago and New York, which drew thousands of spectators. Von Hillern continued solo exhibits of walking one hundred miles around a track in thirteen cities, and one time performed the extraordinary feat of walking 350 miles in six consecutive days and nights.[13] The *Woman's Journal*, a leading women's suffrage newspaper, asserted that her accomplishments refuted Victorian beliefs and medical claims that women were too frail to be full citizens.[14]

In 1878, a middle-aged performer, Ada Anderson, began walking exhibitions. Rather than the one-day walks of von Hillern, hers lasted almost a month and spanned hundreds of miles as she circled a track in the Mozart Garden in Brooklyn. In Chicago, Anderson's exhibition sold more than 24,000 tickets to fans wanting to watch her spectacular proof of women's strength.[15] By 1879, more than one hundred women were walking for money and hundreds of newspapers chronicled these endurance efforts.

For a brief period, women suffragists saw these walkers as symbols for women's rights and the sport received a measure of legitimacy. But the challenge to Victorian morality upset temperance and religious leaders who considered the women pedestriennes as disreputable. "Our modern female pedestrians are a disgrace to themselves and dishonor to society," claimed a letter to the editor of the *Chicago Tribune*, "and an outrageous insult to every virtue which adorns true womanhood."[16]

Controversy also arose over the public brutality of such sporting exhibitions sometimes promoted by unscrupulous, profit-hungry managers, who caused women competitors such as Anderson to walk in agony. This perception heightened public efforts to get the government to stop women's sports for their own protection. Legislation against cockfighting and dog-fighting had already occurred because of cruelty to animals, and some argued that certainly women deserved equal protection from abusive practices.[17] This fueled public disapproval, and the popularity of these events waned. Entrenched Victorian attitudes extolling the myth of women's frailty, despite evidence to the contrary, still prevailed during 1896 when Helga and Clara walked across the continent.

Popular literature and newspaper advertisements caricatured women as the victims of a host of female complaints, and the rise in sales of vegetable compounds such as Lydia Pinkham's marked the era.[18] Exerting a woman's intellect was even suspect. The popular health writer and prestigious doctor, Weir Mitchell, argued that a young woman's "future womanly usefulness was endangered by the steady use of her brain."[19] "New women" challenged these common stereotypes, especially at women's colleges that instituted rigorous physical education programs and active sports, like basketball. For some middle class and wealthy women, horseback riding, cycling, and golf became attractive activities. By wearing the reform costumes, Helga and Clara became identified in the public eye as examples of these new women.

Many doctors, however, perceived that an almost epidemic level of nervous afflictions were caused by these new women seeking greater involvement in public life. One leading male physician in the 1890s warned: "Women's efforts, acted out rashly and foolishly, make her ultimately unfit for active life because of the perilous injury brought on by the deleterious irritations of the outside world."[20] This cultural attitude affected the first group of college-educated women, including Jane Addams, the eventual founder of Hull House in Chicago. Because most professional careers remained closed to educated women, many unemployed postcollege graduates with money took extended trips to Europe on "grand tours" to gain a greater sense of culture. Addams, who took two such tours in her twenties, lamented over this substitute for meaningful work. "I have been idle for two years—I have constantly lost confidence in myself and have gained nothing and improved in nothing."[21]

Theological assumptions that God created women to function in separate spheres from men reinforced these beliefs. Senator George Vest, speaking about women's roles in 1887, expressed the contemporary view: "I do not believe that the Great Intelligence ever intended them to invade the sphere of work given to men, tearing down and destroying all the best influences for which God intended them .... Women are essentially emotional. It is no disparagement to them they are so."[22]

Some society women succumbed to a semi-invalid status, almost a fashionable disease, or endured bed rest strongly recommended by doctors. But women settling the West rarely lived genteel lives. Like Helga's reality on the prairie, their daily survival often demanded physical strength, whether clearing the land with their husbands, tending to several children, farm animals, and a home, or planting and harvesting acres of farmland. When Helga's fall on Riverside Avenue in Spokane led to her earlier bedridden status, she saw no glamour in the confinement. Instead, she risked experimental gynecological surgery to restore her robust health.

Helga's and Clara's actions showed assertiveness, required maximum effort and sweat, aggressiveness, intrepid independence, courage, and sustained physical activity. This journey also immersed them in nature, and the act of walking made them stronger. Traveling through the lonesome land of east Colorado, with the placid South Platte River meandering alongside, the women now contended with temperatures in the 90s. Whistling winds blew prairie dust deep into their clothes. With little human habitation, their companions became white-tail jackrabbits, antelope, prairie dogs, wild range horses, and pheasants. When Helga and Clara paused to rest, they found arrowheads from when the Arapaho and Cheyenne Indians hunted herds of buffalo to feed and clothe their tribes. Now settlers hunted the abundant geese, ducks, deer, and wild turkey. The sharp scent of silver sage, the turbulent moods of the sky, and the yip of a coyote calling its mate helped them endure the monotony of dry grasslands. They trudged northeast through Fort Morgan, Marino, and the abandoned city of Fleming on their route to Sterling. Here they saw the large fields of sugar beets, a major source of income for local farmers' crops.

Always alert, Helga and Clara listened carefully for the dreaded sound of the diamondback, a terrifying rattle in the sandy regions that were "so thick with rattlesnakes as to make it almost impossible to get along."[23] They stepped carefully, always aware of their surroundings. Equally fearsome were the "Mexican cattle," probably longhorns, "that are only afraid of mounted people." As the women followed along the railroad tracks, they used their revolvers freely to protect themselves from the cattle.[24] Earlier pioneers crossed this Overland Trail, many perishing en route as they sought to fulfill their own dreams. Step-by-step Helga and Clara kept trudging along, growing more aware daily of why Americans marveled when they arrived safely at each new destination.

12

AN ELECTRIFYING PRESIDENTIAL ELECTION

Miss (Clara) Estby says she is sick of the trip.
No doubt these two ladies would pull custom like a
span of mules, if any manager here had the nerve to
play them.

—DES MOINES REGISTER
OCTOBER 17, 1896

Helga, now a William Jennings Bryan sup-
porter, shared the excitement of Nebraskans who found
pride in the meteoric rise of interest in their politician
from Lincoln. The women entered Nebraska through
Ogallala. Encouraged by the receptions they received
from governors, Helga decided to visit Bryan's home in
Lincoln and add his important signature to their document. Their trek continued along the South Platte
River, running through the towns of North Platte,
Kearney, and Grand Island, backtracking the Oregon
Trail. Coming from the Pacific Northwest, where the
turbulent crystal water of the Spokane River cut a
dashing swath through the city, this flat muddy river
must have surprised her. Known by locals as a mile
wide and an inch deep, it was even too shallow for nav-

igation, yet wide enough to have islands throughout. But locals knew never to underestimate the river's power; it could be perilously unpredictable.

William McKinley supporters began to question if they had underestimated this other Nebraskan wonder, the thirty-six year old with the silver voice. Because Bryan was young, openly critical of America's major power centers, and lacking the campaign funds and political organization of the far-wealthier Republicans, at first his candidacy seemed as shallow a threat as Nebraska's Platte River. But the currents of his conviction and prodigious energy ran deep. Bryan also tapped into the wellspring of discontent in the agrarian west and south that led to earlier calls for change from the Populist Party. The Populist reformer, Mary Elizabeth Lease, expressed the pent-up anger many felt toward abuse from corporate power. "Wall Street owns the country. It is no longer a government of the people, for the people, by the people, but a government of Wall Street, for Wall Street, and by Wall Street."[1] Bryan carried on this Populist mantle in his own campaign.

Bryan chose to go "to the people," riding the railroads to bring his fiery brand of campaigning to twenty-seven

William and Mary Bryan's home in Lincoln, Nebraska, decorated for a celebration during the Presidential election year of 1896.

Courtesy Nebraska State Historical Society
Photograph Collections, RG3198:22-6.
Detail of this photograph on page 150.

states. Not only farmers wanted to hear him as he barnstormed the country. In Boston, over 75,000 came to listen to him, a sign that sentiment was growing for his "free silver" cause, even in the East.[2] However, it was the heartfelt response he engendered that alarmed his opponents. In Red Cloud, Nebraska, novelist Willa Cather described seeing "rugged, ragged men of the soil weep like children" when he addressed them.[3]

Helga understood. She knew firsthand the economic devastation during President Cleveland's administration and valued Bryan's expressed sympathy with the farmers and working-class families. She witnessed the collapse of the Spokane banks, the foreclosure on businesses and neighbor's farms, and felt her own husband's shame and helplessness at being unable to earn an honest living to support his nine children. Many Bryan supporters saw maintaining the gold standard as a conspiracy of the rich, of Wall Street, and the Republican party wanting to maintain the status quo.[4] William McKinley ardently upheld the gold standard.

Bryan, who once wanted to be a Baptist preacher, used potent religious imagery that electrified his supporters. This also resonated with Helga's Lutheran

Helga favored attorney, orator, and Congressman William Jennings Bryan for president, who was only thirty-six when his Democratic candidacy and concern for the poor galvanized interest in the 1896 election.

Courtesy Nebraska State Historical Society Photograph Collections, RG3198: 17-10.

upbringing and strong knowledge of the Bible. She likely read the newspaper accounts and cartoons that either supported or lambasted his religious rhetoric, especially his famous "Cross of Gold" speech given at the national Democratic Convention. Warming his audience up, he insisted that upholding the gold standard had "slain the poor," and hurt "the producing masses of this nation,"... and the "toilers everywhere." Then, in a thundering conclusion, he railed against big business interests, Republicans, and McKinley, who advocated the gold standard. "We will answer their demand for a gold standard by saying to them: You shall not press down upon the brow of labor this crown of thorns, you shall not crucify mankind upon a cross of gold."[5] This speech threw down the gauntlet of a campaign that riveted the voters throughout the summer and fall of Helga's and Clara's bold venture.

Clara did not share her mother's enthusiasm for Bryan, preferring William McKinley. Republican supporters of McKinley and the gold standard were outraged by what they saw as Bryan's sacrilegious and inflammatory manipulation of sacred Christian symbols. But they, too, couched the election in religious and moral metaphors as they argued against the proposed silver legislation they saw as a disastrous solution. McKinley believed restoring silver in America's coinage would lower the dollar's value to fifty-three cents, thus being an act of "stealing." Many prominent ministers supported the gold standard, and some linked this to

the Ten Commandments, reminding their congrega-
tions, "Thou shalt not steal."[6] Also seeking to appeal to
the anxious working class, McKinley assured a "full
dinner pail" for all citizens, rather than the half pail of
free silver. To repay loans with a reduced-value dollar
would mean cheating the lender, therefore it was "an
issue of integrity and honesty."[7] Keeping the gold standard was essential to revive America's prosperity, the
only "honest dollar" and "sound currency." McKinley
proposed protective tariffs as the best way "to get work
for the masses," which particularly appealed to urban
factory workers in the East. Clara, known for her sen-
sitive gentle spirit, found McKinley's calmer, less divisive campaign more appealing. She looked forward to
going to McKinley's home when they arrived in Ohio.[8]

As Helga and Clara continued their walk on the flat
lands along the Platte River, they saw places where the
Conestoga wagons left their deep wheel ruts, a permanent imprint of the importance of this river that guided
settlers along the Oregon Trail. Helga knew this river
served as a sustaining friend when pioneers journeyed
to Oregon during the 1840s and 50s. But she and Clara
found it cooling, too, as they crossed over three hundred miles to Bryan's home in Lincoln, Nebraska.

When Helga and Clara arrived in Lincoln, Mary
Baird Bryan, the presidential candidate's wife,
warmly welcomed them. He was away campaigning
in the East, but she invited the two for dinner.[9] Helga
and Mary Bryan, almost the same age, shared some

common experiences. Mary also pursued an unconventional course for women when she studied law and took the bar exam, and likely she admired the women's undaunted determination. Both grew up as the only child in their families, and both immensely enjoyed being mothers. But their opportunities as young women in America differed dramatically. At sixteen, when Helga became a mother and wife, Mary entered the Jacksonville Female Academy and graduated as valedictorian in 1881. During her college years, she met William Jennings Bryan, a young attorney, and married him in 1884. By this same year, Helga had dropped out of school, birthed and nurtured four children, and lived in near poverty in a one-room dirt floor sod home. Though women with vastly different economic choices, they still shared the common desire to help their husbands and give their children good futures.

When new opportunities for professional schooling opened for women in America, Mary Bryan, a mother of three, chose to study law. But, "she never dreamed of practicing it." Instead, she saw it as a way to help her husband. "My sole object was to keep pace mentally with Mr. Bryan as far as my ability would permit. I believe that

Mary Baird Bryan welcomed Helga and Clara into her home for dinner and bought several pictures. Her husband, William Jennings Bryan, was away campaigning.

Courtesy Nebraska State Historical Society Photograph Collection, RG3198: 2-8.

this is the only way in which a wife can keep the affection and sympathy of an intellectual husband."[10] She took the bar exam both in the District and Supreme Courts of Nebraska, something rarely done by women. Instead of practicing law, she became active in women's clubs, especially Sorosis, which encouraged thought among women. An enthusiastic advocate for college education for women, she likely encouraged Clara, who was bright and articulate, to consider college if they received the $10,000. Before Helga and Clara left, Mary bought several pictures and added her signature to the document.[11]

From Lincoln, they walked northeast to Omaha. Here Helga and Clara saw the grand Missouri River and a flourishing town for trade and commerce. But in Omaha, Clara fell sick, perhaps from food poisoning. Unfortunately, this laid them up for several days, causing Helga to revise their expected arrival date to December 13, providing allowance for illness as the contract stipulated. Now into September, they still had several states to cross before reaching Manhattan.

When Clara felt better, good fortune aided them as temperatures hovering near the 70s created a far better climate for walking. Along the riverbanks, they could

---

To earn money along the route, Helga and Clara sold formal portraits of themselves, an effective fundraiser.

Courtesy Portch/Bahr Family Photograph Collection.

C. S. Ricker,

1313 Wash. Ave. S. Minneapolis.

rest under the shade of the cottonwoods, and finding meals, housing, and work became easier in these more populated areas. They stayed in Atlantic, Iowa, the home of the Rock Island Railroad depot, and then followed the tracks east. Wearing straw hats to protect themselves from the sun, they passed by rural family farms and Midwestern towns that exuded a sense of peace and stability. As Helga and Clara's accomplishment of traversing halfway across the United States became known, reporters took interest in their expected arrivals into a new town. On October 15, the *Des Moines Leader* reported that the women were somewhere between Atlantic and Des Moines after having covered almost 2800 miles already. The reporter described their short gray skirts "reaching only to their shoe tops," heavy shoes, and leggings, and said they should be arriving soon to sell pictures of themselves to earn money.[12]

Then, early frosts and cold weather in October sabotaged Iowa farmers and gave Helga a vivid reminder of the vulnerability of farmers everywhere. What looked bucolic belied the full truth. With the onset of cold weather, the market demand for watermelons abruptly ended and thousands of beautiful ripened melons rotted in the fields south of Des Moines. Like the ways a hailstorm or grasshopper infestation destroyed crops in Minnesota and unseasonable rains ruined the grain fields near Mica Creek, she knew intimately how such crop failures sank farm families deeper in debt.

They followed the Rock Island Railroad through Dexter to Des Moines where they arrived on October 17 and stayed at the Savery Hotel. After announcing Helga's and Clara's arrival and the $10,000 wager, the *Des Moines Register* reporter noted that they were "being watched by agents of the woman who has made the offer and therefore prevented from stealing rides," and that they continued to have confidence in their eventual success. "They said last night that they expected to win it."[13]

The reporter also mentioned that in addition to the wager, the women were writing a book of their experiences. From their early interviews in Washington, through to the final interviews in the East, Helga attached importance to her plans to write a book. An avid reader, she expressed confidence in her ability to capture this intrepid journey. But, she saw this in addition to winning the $10,000. Although probably Helga's original idea, not the sponsors', they may have agreed to help her make essential contacts in the New York publishing world. Helga also stated that the purpose of the feat they were attempting to perform "on the part of the lady who is putting up the $10,000 is to demonstrate the endurance of women." Helga and Clara clearly demonstrated this strength. But Helga makes it equally clear that this was *not* what motivated her to walk. The controversy between "new women" and those advocating that women need to live a protected life were not her concerns. As she stated their purpose to the reporter, "as far as they are concerned it is to earn the $10,000."[14]

They worked odd jobs in Des Moines long enough to replenish their depleted funds and to buy new shoes and mackintosh raincoats. Cinders on the railroad tracks quickly destroyed their shoes, so now they planned to walk along the dirt roads beside the Rock Island Railroad into Chicago. By now Helga no longer lived with so many of the fears that people planted in her mind before she left. Instead of threats, almost every day in their encounters with ordinary citizens, men and women alike, they received kindness. Most people wanted to help them. As an Iowa reporter wrote, "They say, however, that their reception has always been satisfactory and that they have had no troubles."[15] Even so, the article concluded with reference to Clara's candid comment, "Miss Estby said she was sick of the trip."[16]

Before leaving town, they met with Governor Francis M. Drake and he added his signature to their document.[17] Frustrated by the delays and needing to raise money with as brief a stay as possible, Helga began writing ahead to towns, asking them to set them up in a public place where they could tell their story and sell photographs. On October 22, when Helga and Clara traveled through Marengo, Helga wrote a letter to the Davenport, Iowa, newspaper. She announced that they expected to be there the following Tuesday, October 27. She wanted to know how much the manager of the opera house would be willing to pay her and her daughter to come there "as an advertisement," intimating that

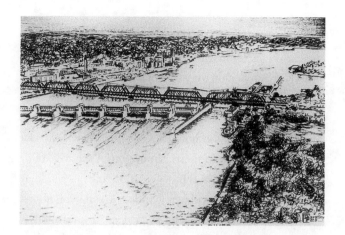

The two walkers cross the Mississippi at Davenport, Iowa, on the brand-new railroad and wagon bridge.

Courtesy Rock Island Arsenal Museum.

they needed to make their expenses en route. Anticipating her arrival, the October 24 *Davenport Democrat* reporter wrote that the city will be "honored" by her call: "We hereby refer the matter to the managers of the many places of amusement in this city. No doubt these two ladies would pull custom like a span of mules, if any manager here had the nerve to play them."[18]

Shortly outside of Marengo, Helga and Clara passed the experimental Amana Colonies. These German communities that sought religious freedom and the opportunity to practice their distinctive communal farming system settled along the Iowa River in 1855. Rather than live on isolated farm homesteads as Helga and Ole did outside Canby, all the farm families lived within the village and contributed to creating a self-sustaining community. Each person over school age held assigned tasks in the kitchens, fields, factories, or shops. Helga and Clara admired the craftsmanship of the sturdy timber and native sandstone homes, and they knew that Ole would have shared in their admiration of the well-built homes, shops, and churches—even the barrels made at the cooperage. The villages exuded a sense of abundance, with bountiful vegetable gardens, beautiful flowers, and grape vines climbing up each house arbor. It is possible that women invited Helga and Clara to a meal in the common dining areas where the women cooked together and then ate in quiet contemplation at tables separate from the men. A farm feast of homemade breads, hams, and berry wines would have energized them for the next stretch ahead. Or they may have been shunned, seen as a worldly influence, unfit for associating with the children and women.

They walked along the Millrace, a seven-mile canal used to power the Amana Woolen Mill, a major source of revenue for the villagers. Seeing women leisurely boating and hearing the laughter of children playing with their mothers along the waterway inevitably brought memories of family outings by the Spokane River and picnics in the parks. In the silent hours of walking, Helga's mind often drifted to images of Ole and each of her children and a longing for the familiar comforts of home. Almost every single day in the last twenty years, motherhood had shaped the rhythms of her life. Tucking children into bed, reading them stories, and listening to their daily pleasures and worries provided joy amid the labor of caring for a family of eleven. Even with all their difficulties, she had felt a comfort in these familiar family patterns.

Now each day brought something new, challenging her in unexpected ways. She liked that walking had made her stronger and liked having time for lingering discussions with Clara and all those who befriended them. On some days, she even enjoyed the many hours of solitude in nature and the time for reflection, something she rarely knew when caring constantly for children. But the family was so far away, and she missed them each and every day.

When Helga and Clara arrived in Davenport and saw the sheer size of the famous muddy Mississippi, it provided visual proof they were over their halfway mark. In 1896, a marvelous new steel government bridge connected Arsenal Island to Davenport, Iowa, replacing the old iron bridge. Clara fell ill again for a brief time, adding one more delay. But soon they crossed the river, joining the pedestrians and teams of horses that walked on the ground level while trains roared overhead. Destined for even more densely populated land, they knew finding food and shelter should no longer be a problem. However, Helga now carried a new worry as she wondered if the good weather, so essential for their success, would hold.

13

EARNING THEIR OWN WAY

*They are certainly a strong testimony of woman's
endurance and ability to care for herself.*

—PLYMOUTH (INDIANA) REPUBLIC
NOVEMBER 19, 1896

For the first time since crossing the western
mountain ridges, Helga and Clara encountered snowstorms as they walked toward Chicago. With the
chilling winds and sharp drop in temperatures, their
short wool mackintosh jackets gave them limited protection from freezing weather.

On the plains near Chicago, hoboes tried to accost
them, following the women for three-fourths of a mile.
"Clara and I walked backward pointing our revolvers at
them to save ourselves from harm," stated Helga.
Clara shot them in the face with her pepper gun, an
insect powder box filled with cayenne pepper and "the
cayenne made them desist." The tramps that attempted
to molest them "begged for mercy."[1]

During their rush to Chicago, the culminating days
of the Presidential election reached a fever pitch. By
the day American's cast their ballot, Bryan had trav-

eled over 18,000 miles and given 600 speeches.[2] While Bryan's campaign took him directly to the voters, McKinley brought hundreds of thousands of voters directly to him in a "front-porch" campaign. Also wanting that face-to-face contact with voters, McKinley conducted a steady campaign at his home in Canton, Ohio. In well-orchestrated visits, delegations converged on Canton from many states, brought in through the support of the railroad barons. In these festive visits, replete with welcoming brass band fanfare, McKinley presented his platform to over 750,000 persons, including thirty delegations on one day when he gave fourteen formal speeches.[3] Delegates liked the distinguished Civil War veteran's calm appeal to reason and common sense. As a former United States congressman and governor of Ohio, he offered mature experience to voters. He stressed building unity and harmony in the nation, not social or regional conflicts.

The Republican party also had a far richer campaign coffer which enabled them to print over two hundred million brochures and pamphlets to promote McKinley.[4] Major corporations contributed to assure that McKinley and the gold standard won, including $500,000 from Standard Oil and J.P. Morgan alone. This exceeded the entire amount of the Democrat's fund.[5]

On November 3, when Helga and Clara were just southwest of Chicago, they witnessed one of the largest election turnouts in the United States. Nearly eighty percent of eligible voters came to the polls.[6] To Clara's delight, McKinley won decisively by around six hundred thousand votes. Bryan's message, however, resonated with well over six million Americans, and he won in twenty-two states, including most of the West and all of the South. Although big money clearly helped McKinley win the election, other important factors appealed to citizens. His personal character and his reasoned message that promised stability, rather than the dangerous experiment with free silver, appealed to urban Northeasterners and even many Midwest voters.

As they neared the outskirts of America's great Midwest city, where the Great Lakes link with the Mississippi River system, dirty smog hovered in the horizon from the factories of industrial America, a startling change from the clear skies of the plains. Shanties housing the poor stretched into long slums along the route into Chicago.[7]

Needing to live on the least amount of money possible, Helga and Clara arrived in Chicago on November 7, "footsore and travel stained," with only a dime to their name and "their clothes about in rags." The *Chicago Evening Post* announced their $10,000 tramp, and noted "the women are poorly clad and will make an effort to secure money in the city to purchase winter clothing before proceeding further."[8] To replenish their funds, Helga and Clara modeled their reform costumes in a progressive department store, a novel change from the washing and cleaning they did in the West. They earned enough for much-needed new outfits and shoes.[9]

Chicago illustrated in a microcosm the extremes of wealth and poverty in the United States that the presidential election highlighted. In the heart of Chicago's resplendent commercial district near the beautiful Lake Michigan shore, Helga and Clara saw the abundant wealth concentrated in the bustling business center. Barges carrying grain, coal, salt, iron ore, limestone, and steel exemplified the powerful transportation role the great inland port played in the world. The department store where they modeled their reform dresses carried the latest high fashions for Chicago's rich society women. Designers created elegant Victorian dresses and hats with exquisite fabrics from around the world, sewn with yards and yards of organdy, lace, silks, satins, heather wools, furs, and feathers. As a seamstress, Helga was fascinated by the sheer abundance of beautiful textures and cloth.

Yet, like in most industrial urban centers in America, the financial Panic of 1893 threw thousands of capable Chicago working-class men and their families into destitution and despair. Over 100,000 remained out of work in the winter of 1893–94, yet transients continued to ride the boxcars into the city in search of jobs.[10] These men, unable to find employment, ended up in flophouses or homeless on the streets. A burgeoning immigrant population from Europe poured into the city, too, often living in crowded, disease-ridden tenements. This contributed to the outbreak of diphtheria that occurred during the month of Helga and Clara's visit, with over 5,000 diagnosed with the disease.[11]

These destructive conditions affecting the lives of many of America's newest immigrants drew the abiding interest of Jane Addams, a young woman who began a settlement house amid the urban misery of Chicago's slums in 1889. Born in America the same year as Helga, Jane benefited from the new educational opportunities for women and attended Rockford College in Illinois. An excellent student with a strong moral code, but physically frail, she longed to be "useful" in the world. After graduation, however, very few professional occupations were open for educated women.

During her early twenties, while Helga was gaining confidence homesteading on the prairie, Jane often lamented that the idle leisure life of privileged women left them with no significant work to do. In her early twenties, after back surgery ended her medical school ambitions, Jane traveled twice to Europe on "grand tours," a favorite diversion for women of means in the late nineteenth century. Often traveling for a year or more to pursue culture by visiting museums, seeing theater and opera, learning languages, or going on shopping sprees, it also provided a means to fend off boredom or depression. However, after an encounter with the wretchedness of urban poverty in East London, she visited Toynbee Hall. Educated young men in England lived and worked here, striving to ease the life of the poorest in the East End, and this model became a catalyst to Addams' solution of something useful to do.

She returned to Chicago and founded Hull House with her friend, Ellen Gates Starr. As with Helga's choice to walk across America, Addams' choice to live amid the poor was unheard of in her era. But she insisted that this work "saved" those who were serving, giving educated women like herself meaningful work, as much as it helped immigrants. Living among Italian, Polish, Greek, Russian, and Bohemian immigrants, the women in Hull House offered friendship and services for their neighbors. They opened kindergarten and daycare facilities for children of working mothers, an employment bureau, art gallery, playgrounds, libraries, and classes.

By the time Helga and Clara came to Chicago, Addams' innovative efforts as a social reformer were becoming well-known. As she saw the wretched living and working conditions of her neighbors, she wrote and spoke persuasively for more humane and just conditions. She also befriended influential clergymen who taught that Christians needed to help change the unjust structures that brutalized the vulnerable, not just provide individual charity after the fact. This "social gospel" offered an intellectual and spiritual framework for Addams' efforts to abolish child labor and to improve conditions in unsafe factories, sordid tenements, and garbage-filled streets.[12]

Even during the depressed years of the 1890s, Chicago manifested the raucous confidence of a pivotal city standing on the brink of a new era at the turn of a century. Despite the nation's financial collapse, Chicago hosted over twenty million visitors at the 1893 World's Columbian Exposition, financing a 586-acre tribute to American ingenuity. This fair demonstrated the newest technological wonders for farms, factories, and homes, reassuring nervous Americans to expect a positive future. It even included a Women's Building exhibition that highlighted women designers, scientists, writers, architects, and artists; it was here that many women were first introduced to bicycle skirts like the ones Helga and Clara wore.

Helga's contract stipulation only required they visit mayors after they arrived in Chicago, so they made their way to the mayor's office in City Hall. Here Mayor George E. Swift's "Private Secretary Minkler" signed their credentials for the mayor to show they had visited the city.[13] The *Chicago Journal*, also featuring Helga and Clara's arrival on page one of the newspaper, stated that the $10,000 reward was "offered by a New York weekly syndicate," probably referring to the *New York World* that first announced their trip.[14] Now accounting for illness, Helga states that "to accommodate this feat" they must walk twenty-nine miles a day to reach New York by December 13, actually an overestimation of the mileage.

Cold, bone-chilling days lay ahead as they left the windy city and traveled through the increasingly populated states of Indiana and Ohio. On November 14, they walked twenty-five miles from Hanna, Indiana, to Plymouth, Indiana. Coming into town hungry and tired on a Saturday evening at 8:15, they stopped at the Ross House and asked for supper and accommodations. They were so browned by the sun and exposure to the weather that "Landlord Bowel" held some doubts as to "whether he was being imposed upon by some Gypsies or tramp women." But he became intrigued with his guests and notified a reporter from the *Plymouth Republic* who wrote a lengthy article on the women and their wager.[15] For the first time, an article mentioned "a wealthy lady of Spokane, Washington" who wanted to test women's physical endurance, as well as her ability to provide for herself, had "made an offer."[16] A wealthy Spokane woman connected to the "eastern sponsor" might have known Helga, provided the contact with Spokane's mayor, and paid the money for the formal portraits taken in Spokane to send to the *New York World* newspaper.

In these populated areas, Helga and Clara were now earning enough by selling their photographs to

When earning travel funds by cooking, cleaning, and sewing took up too much time, Helga began writing ahead to city newspapers seeking opportunities to speak and sell their pictures.

nearly meet expenses, which so far, totaled around $195. Interested in their physical appearance and short skirts, the reporter noted that "smoke and dust was grimed into their necks," but admitted "little else could be expected from following the railroad for so many months." Observing the women were "of medium height and would probably weigh 112 or 115 pounds," they "seemed only slightly fatigued" after walking twenty-five miles from Hanna. Even their hairstyle garnered attention, perhaps to show news-paper readers how "normal" or feminine Helga and Clara seemed. "The women have brown hair, the mother doing hers up in a knot while that of the daughter is frizzed or curled." The fact they had worn out seven pairs of shoes each and wore a rain-proof gossamer or mackintosh as their only wrap also interested this thorough reporter.

Clearly impressed with their journey, the reporter concluded, "While they were not at all backward as ladies, they were not immodest, and seemed to have the respect of those who met them. They are certainly a strong testimony of woman's endurance and ability to care for herself."[17]

The women reached Atwood, Indiana, on Sunday, November 15, and spent the night. Walking along the Pittsburgh Railway for almost fifty miles to Fort Wayne, they arrived on Wednesday, November 18. They checked into the Bradley Grand Central Hotel and spent the evening at the major drugstore in town where "quite a number of photographs were sold in the city." "As only 800 miles remain to be traveled," stated the reporter from the *Fort Wayne Sentinel* who became convinced of their eventual success, "Mrs. Estby and her daughter already have the prize assured them."[18]

Once again, a reporter speaks of a Spokane connection but with a new twist. "This long journey was the conception of a wealthy woman of Spokane, who is an ardent advocate of woman's suffrage, and it is intended to test the power of woman's endurance."[19] Never before has Helga mentioned a connection to women's suffrage, although she consistently refers to the goal of proving the endurance of women. In an earlier interview with the *Idaho Statesman*, she mentioned they were walking to New York on a wager "put up by parties who do not care to have their names divulged until we reach our destination."[20] The female sponsors appeared to keep their identity secret even from Helga, a term she accepted. For whatever reasons, these sponsors encouraged Helga and Clara to gamble with their very lives, engaging them in a desperate feat.

14

A Rush to the Finish

They are so anxious to gain time that they made no stop here at all.

—OHIO STATE JOURNAL
UPPER SANDUSKY, NOVEMBER 24, 1896

They called on President-elect McKinley at Canton last evening and were genially welcomed by the Major and his pleasant wife.

—ALLIANCE DAILY REVIEW
NOVEMBER 30, 1896

When Helga first proposed the walk across America, she heard all the negative predictions. "It's an impossible trip." "Women can't do such a thing." "You won't survive." But as she continued east, she found that with their unique story and engaging personalities, people were anxious to help them along the way. Furthermore, Helga's worthy ambition to save a family home fit a Victorian value, even if her method appeared radical. By the time Helga and Clara entered the last few hundred miles of their trip, winding through eastern Ohio and the Amish countryside of Pennsylvania, the women undoubtedly felt a high sense of achievement and relief. Even Clara, sick of the trip by the time they arrived in the Midwest, seemed excited about their accomplishment, or at least that the end was drawing near.

Some reporters noted the women's swinging emotional pendulum. Although Helga expressed assurance that they would make their destination, it was now coupled with a nagging fear that the sponsor might void the contract if they arrived after the December destination date. Delay caused by Clara's ankle injury and illness placed them in a race against the calendar. Even after walking a formidable thirty-eight miles in one day to make up lost time, they still lagged a few days behind schedule. Surviving the summer dangers of desert heat exhaustion had changed to surviving December's chilling winds and snowstorms. Recalling the 1880 Minnesota winter that began in mid-October, Helga knew they needed unseasonably mild weather on their side. A winter storm paralyzing the East would make walking in November and December impossible. Would their luck hold?

A brief November 24 article in Upper Sandusky's, *Ohio State Journal* indicated their anxiety and hurry as they reached eastern Ohio. No longer did they have the leisure to stop, rest, and earn money. "They are so anxious to gain time that they made no stop here at all," lamented a reporter, perhaps disappointed not to meet the globetrotters.[1] However, while in Ohio, they did take time to visit "General Keep-Off-the-Grass"

Helga and Clara stopped in Massillon, Ohio, and visited Jacob Coxey. His "army" of unemployed men walked to the Capitol in Washington in 1894 seeking government support of a public-works project to provide men with work, setting a precedent for future non-violent protests on the Capitol grounds.

Coxey, a friend of laborers, in Massillon. Jacob Coxey, a wealthy man who owned a sandstone quarry in Ohio, ranches, and race horses, traveled the poor Midwest roads that alternated between frozen, muddy, or dusty. He believed that if the United States wanted to grow and prosper again, it needed to fix the dilapidated roads, so he began a Good Roads Association.[2]

Then, troubled by the massive unemployment of 1893 that left men desperately in need of work, he came up with an innovative but controversial idea. Why not have the United States government create public work jobs and hire unemployed workers to fix America's roads? After walking these same troublesome roads, Helga and Clara understood exactly what he meant. Through his Ohio representatives he petitioned Congress for a $500 million public works bill; it languished, ignored by legislators. To draw attention to his petition, he devised a strategic march with another free-silver cohort he had met at the Chicago World's Fair. During the depth of the depression in 1894, they invited out-of-work men to leave Massillon, Ohio, on Easter Sunday to join in a four-hundred-mile march to the nation's Capitol steps, aiming for a May 1 arrival. Newspapers from around the country, intrigued with this novel protest from decent men desperate for work, sent journalists to accompany this first group of 122 marchers who called themselves the "Commonweal of Christ."[3] Reporters provided colorful daily news throughout the spring, which spawned offshoots of other groups, and Coxey's Army swelled to four hundred. They represented a variety of occupations, various unions, and even a few from fraternal organizations like the Odd Fellows and Masons; their fellow members often gave them help along the way.

Other groups joined them on May 1 for this unique demonstration. Unemployed men from the West gathered to take trains east, legally and illegally, to show their solidarity. With so many people in America affected by the depression, the usually peaceful Coxeyites found sympathetic support for their plight and petition. In Pittsburgh, four hundred members of the Iron Moulders' Union helped create a parade, marching in front of them, complete with a band.[4] Although the poorly clad men often marched with little to eat, sometimes supporters provided meals as well as encouragement for the marchers.

It is probable that Helga knew of the Coxey groups from the Washington State coast who collected in Spokane during May of 1894. Hundreds of men stayed in the city for several days, putting on benefits to explain their mission and raise funds for the trip East, and even playing baseball games with locals.[5] As a union worker, her husband may have met with the marchers. The strategies Coxeyites had used on their marches might have planted seeds for Helga when she began planning her transcontinental journey. She had seen how the heavy utilization of newspaper publicity helped these men gain popular support and tangible items, like a good meal or shelter for a night. Though internal conflicts and poor leadership undermined and ultimately disbanded these Northwest efforts, Coxey's original group arrived six weeks later in Washington, D.C., and camped on the outskirts. Unarmed, poorly clad, often hungry, the men marched with a simple hope that the U.S. government might recognize an opportunity to assist the desperately poor in the country. They did not ask for a handout, just a chance to do honest work.

President Cleveland's administration, fearful of trouble and riots, refused to grant the Coxeyites a permit to march the last few miles to the Capitol steps. Coxey argued that the Capitol steps were public property and it was his constitutional right to speak. After his men had walked four hundred miles, although he often rode in a carriage, he was determined to carry their message to the legislature. They marched into the city, with more than 20,000 curious spectators there to greet them or perhaps, to observe the potential confrontation. Over three hundred policeman stood guard by the Capitol.[6] Police shoved Coxey down the Capitol steps before he could give his speech, eventually arresting him for "unauthorized parading on the grass" and "carrying signs on the Capitol grounds," a charge ridiculed by some newspapers as overkill.[7]

Newspapers in Spokane followed this first major march of common citizens going to the Capitol to petition for change. One West Coast reporter argued that the nation should be proud of Coxey's Army, that they showed the strength of the nation when the dispossessed demonstrated responsibly. "These men who feel themselves wronged do not propose to kill and overthrow—they do not march with guns—they do not threaten—they appeal—they petition—they protest—they reason."[8] In reality, they acted out of faith that congress held the power to fulfill the Pledge of Allegiance's lofty promise of justice for all.

Helga told reporters that Coxey "gave them some valuable pointers on marching." Yet, he only walked part of the four hundred miles from Massillon, Ohio, to Washington, D.C., taking off in his carriage to conduct business when necessary. By now, Helga and Clara had walked over twenty-five hundred miles. Before they left, he added his signature to the growing list of impressive Americans who signed Helga's introductory letter.[9]

On Sunday, November 29, they walked from Massillon to Canton, hopeful for a visit with the President-elect William McKinley. Now it was Clara's turn to be excited when Major and Mrs. McKinley invited the women in for an hour's visit. "Clara felt most welcomed here."[10] A respected Civil War major, McKinley studied law and then entered political life, eventually becoming governor of Ohio. His wife, Ida Saxton, once a beautiful young woman given all the advantages of a fine education and travel, suffered from years of poor health. After the death of her two young daughters, her only children, she became a semi-invalid and appeared to struggle with phlebitis and epileptic seizures.[11] She still was considered a "charming hostess," and Helga and Clara said the President-elect and his wife "encouraged" the women on their journey. They added their prestigious signatures to the document of introduction, and he verified their arrival by adding, "The ladies bearing this paper called at my home, Canton, Ohio, Sunday evening, November 29, 1896."[12]

The Spokane *Spokesman-Review* learned of the President-elect's warm welcome to the women and

The new President-elect William McKinley on his famous porch in Canton, Ohio. On Sunday evening, November 29, 1896, Helga and Clara spent an hour at their home.

Courtesy Ohio Historical Society, Collection P356, box 9, folder 1.

published an article titled "Spokane's Caller at McKinley's." For a local woman to be received by the President-elect in his home merited her hometown's attention. Stating that Mrs. Estby "will be well remembered in this city," the reporter recalled the $10,000 prize from "some generous old lady of New York" that motivated the walk and the requirement "to wear a peculiar style of dress," which they will take on the lecture circuit after completing their journey.[13] Then, a hint of the local reporter's attitude toward Helga's unconventional actions emerged. When elab-

After the death of two daughters and the onset of epileptic seizures, Ida Saxton McKinley lived most of her adult life as an invalid. She still served as a charming First Lady, receiving guests while remaining seated in a blue velvet chair.

orating on her family, the reporter notes that several children are left at the home in Mica Creek "with their father who is quietly cultivating the ranch while his wife and eldest daughter are tramping across the country to win wealth and fame." The reporter, however, did acknowledge the reasons motivating her venture. "There is a mortgage on the ranch, and while the father is trying to raise enough to feed the family, the mother will try to raise the mortgage." Helga's understanding of the "art of advertising," and her success in getting interviewed in every city of

Major William McKinley conducted his successful "front porch campaign" from his home. McKinley's railroad supporters brought thousands of delegates to his porch.

any size she visited, seemed to intrigue the writer. "It is clear that she has pluck, for she has accomplished what she started out to do, and when she reaches New York will have enough press clippings to give her a good salary in a museum."[14] Her hometown newspaper in Spokane Falls now used the word "when" instead of "if" she arrives in New York, clearly impressed that she was nearing her goal.

On the following day, a reporter from the *Alliance Daily Review* in Alliance, Ohio, interviewed Helga and Clara as they passed through the city in the afternoon. Too much in a hurry to stop, the reporter "met the ladies in the west yards and walked with them to Freedom Street." After first observing that "both are quite intelligent," the reporter described Clara, noticing "that the latter is quite good looking."[15] Clearly still enthused at the generous reception they received at the President-elect's, the reporter commented that "Mrs. Estby and daughter were highly pleased with their treatment at the home of the McKinleys" and assumed "they are both ardent Republicans." Recognizing sickness and an accident "have thrown them behind somewhat," the reporter explained the $10,000 wager, the looming deadline, and their determined spirits, stating simply, "They expect to win it."[16]

In two days, they planned to be in Pittsburgh, Pennsylvania, a major milestone and the beginning of their last major state to traverse. With each day bringing them closer to their goal, which now seemed very viable, their excitement grew.

15

THE IMPOSSIBLE HAPPENS

Mrs. Estby fears that the woman with whom the wager was made will refuse to pay the $10,000.... that the daughter's sprained ankle will not be allowed to count as sickness.

—NEW YORK WORLD
DECEMBER 24, 1896

Almost two weeks later, in early December, the dusty, "tired, but brave" mother and daughter arrived in Sewickly, Pennsylvania. The local newspaper described Clara as "sprightly," and noticed she "did not appear to dread the remaining distance." Helga, seen as a "slight built, but a determined-looking woman," presented the signatures of governors and officials of all the states and cities through which they had passed as proof they had visited these places. Each new destination strengthened Helga's sense of achievement as she reiterated her confidence to the reporter. "Mrs. Espey [*sic*] was confident she would reach her destination on time and carry off the $10,000 prize."[1]

In western Pennsylvania, men began to harass the mother and daughter, exactly what others warned them about before they left Spokane. Walking through coal-mining country, the miners and highwaymen threatened them so constantly, Helga said "they didn't hesitate to brandish their revolvers." After rarely encountering trouble with other "tramps" along the journey, they told a Lebanon, Pennsylvania, reporter that "people were much too lenient with them here."[2]

They walked from Pittsburgh to Harrisburg, where they visited Governor Daniel Hastings in the capitol building. Because the contract required only the signatures of mayors after Chicago, they must have enjoyed the receptions they received if they chose to drop in on the governor. Then they traveled through the Pennsylvania Dutch county of Berks. Here the people treated them "exceptionally well and showed them very marked attention."[3] These Amish and Mennonite farmers fled to America from Germany and Switzerland so they could practice their religion without fear. They developed a peaceful land, where the patchwork of neatly laid out farms reflected the settlers' industry and care. The kindnesses they gave Helga and Clara inevitably included meals from their productive crops. However, "the strange dialect spoken by the natives almost caused the westerners to die of laughter."[4]

Jubilation mixed with anxiety as their deadline loomed. Helga and Clara took a rare opportunity to ride on a trolley after they left Hummelstown at 6 o'clock in the morning. They rode through Annville, Lebanon, and on to Myerstown, "from where they were obliged to walk to Womelsdorf, when they could take the trolley again." Mrs. Estby said, "Among the stipulations of the contract we made are that we must not beg and [we can] either walk or ride on electric cars."[5]

Possibly the contract allowed the electric car rides because of safety factors within industrial cities. Or perhaps it was a "free ride," thus not breaking the stipulation against paying for rides. Other than the free wagon ride near Walla Walla, this was the only time they admitted not walking. Clearly, time pressures made them hurry at this point. However, as this ride occurred in a very public environment, and Helga herself reported the ride to a journalist she knew was writing up their story, it was unlikely they risked breaking their contract.

Rising excitement about the enormity of these women's achievement led to even socialites welcoming them when they arrived in Reading, Pennsylvania, on December 19. They stayed at the Hotel Penn where they received numerous callers, "including some well-known society people."[6] They recounted their experiences "most entertainingly," and the women, though bronzed by exposure, were otherwise "looking none the worse for their exploits." The *Reading Times* reporter concluded, "The girdlers feel jubilant over the near approach of the completion of their journey."[7]

Now within striking distance of their long-sought goal, when the two reached Phillipsburg, New Jersey,

*Numerous callers, including some "well-known society people,"
came to the Hotel Penn in Reading, Pennsylvania, to meet the astonishing women.*

somebody misdirected them through Morristown.
They walked forty-five miles off their course, "a
grievous mistake that caused them to be caught in
last night's storm," noted the *New York World*. So
close to fulfilling their dream after seven months of
exertion and more than 3500 miles, the weary women
returned to the right road and pressed on toward New
York City. "When they reached Jersey City this
forenoon they were happy. They saw the tall buildings of New York and knew that their journey was
nearly at an end."[8]

Shortly after 1 o'clock on December 23, seven
months and 18 days after they left Spokane, Helga and

Clara set foot on Manhattan Island. To reach their destination, the *World* newspaper office, required only a few minutes. What triumphant thoughts surged through Helga and Clara as they stepped into this newspaper building—the same publisher that first announced their intentions last April 26? Did they window shop on the city streets as they walked downtown, imagining what glorious Christmas gifts they could bring home to the family? The reporter caught a hint of their impatient delight, "The elevators were slow to carry them upstairs, they thought, so eager were they to end their journey."[9]

Impressed with the mental abilities and physical appearance of the winsome women, the reporter expressed amazement over the wonder of their achievement, stating that Mrs. Estby and her daughter were "the only women who ever walked across the continent." Helga was described as an "intelligent, very witty, good conversationalist" and a well-educated thirty-eight year old who has traveled considerably. The enamored writer also observed that she is "in excellent physical condition and lost only one pound on the journey." Clara, now nineteen, was described as a well-educated graduate of a Spokane high school "with a full round face and sparkling blue eyes and ... a plump, well-developed figure." A full description of their walking outfits included: bicycle skirts, reaching a few inches below their knees; stout cycle shoes with boot tops encased their

feet; short black coats buttoned closely to the neck; low-crowned alpine hats; and warm woolen gloves.[10] Whatever internal triumph Helga felt that day appeared to be shadowed by anxiety, fearful that the woman who made the wager might refuse to pay the $10,000 because they missed the stipulated deadline.

Helga and Clara's feat attracted the attention of several other New York daily newspapers. Like in earlier news articles, reporters expressed strong interest in the fact that two women earned over $300 for the trip expenses through their own labor, noting that their work stops "aggregated to around two months." On Christmas Eve, the *New York Times* reported on this remarkable performance for women, acknowledging that "a pedestrian trip from the Pacific to the Atlantic is a big task for men, but when women perform it, it becomes remarkable." Then several paragraphs described the wager, the particular difficulties they overcame with highwaymen, storms, and Clara's ankle accident. But the *New York Times'* strongest fascination appeared to be in the impressive stature of signatures the women garnered along the way. Besides President and Mrs. William McKinley, Mrs. William Jennings Bryan, and "Gen-

---

Helga and Clara arrived at the New York World *newspaper building in New York City Hall Park, on December 23, 1896, jubilant at their achievement.*

eral" Coxey, the signatures included many of America's leading governors and mayors.[11]

The *New York Herald* also covered their feat and added news on their contract and concerns. After referring to the ten-day delay caused by Clara's sprained ankle, information was included on their extreme efforts to make up this lost time. "By forced marches, the women were able to make up six days of the ten." The question loomed over whether the wealthy sponsor would quibble over the delay caused by Clara's ankle sprain and not count these days as sickness. This "will have to be settled before the travelers know whether they win or lose the wager."[12]

Wire services picked up these articles and the Christmas Eve *Spokane Chronicle* and the *Spokesman-Review* announced their safe arrival and successful achievement, most likely the first time their family and friends learned of their stunning accomplishment. After covering their accomplishment, the *Spokesman-Review* admitted that "it was not generally believed the proposed trip would be completed" when they left last spring. The reporter noted that Mrs. Estby left a husband in Mica Creek to take care of the balance of the family while "the two female globe-trotters are out for the alleged wager." Then the reporter added a commentary on Spokane community attitudes toward Helga's character and reputation. "Mrs. Estby, though regarded as rather peculiar, was a determined woman, and when she said she was going to walk to New York,

An artist for the New York World *newspaper drew this sketch of Helga's and Clara's astounding achievement, which was published on Christmas day, 1896.*

those who knew her said she would carry out the determination. Doubt, however, exists about the $10,000 which she said she was to receive."[13]

The Estbys always celebrated Christmas Eve with a festive Norwegian dinner, with the special preparation of *lefse*, sour cream pudding with lingonberry sauce, *lutefisk*, and almond cookies made by Helga. December of 1896 was a lonely Christmas for Ole and the seven children. Ole knew more than anyone the truth of the observations that Helga was "peculiar, but determined." He had seen his wife, bedridden with pain just five years earlier, boldly risk innovative surgery to restore her health and then exert the physical strength to walk across America. But now the world knew they were delinquent on taxes and in danger of losing their farm, an embarrassing truth for this hard-working husband and father. The local newspaper article also may have raised Ole's fears that all his wife's heroic efforts might have been in vain.

Late on Christmas Eve afternoon, Helga and Clara returned to the *World* newspaper with troubling news. Somehow, after being in New York City less than four hours, they had lost all their money. What worried Helga most was not that she lost her money but that "the pocketbook contained most of the diary of her trip." The pocketbook had Mrs. Estby's Spokane address in it, and that of her present home on No. 6 Rivington Street.[14]

Perhaps because health promoters in the 1890s, such as Lydia Pinkham, urged women to drink various herbal and other vegetable compounds to gain strength for their frail bodies, the reporter added, "The daughter never drank anything but milk. The mother allowed herself but one cup of coffee a day. Neither of them took stronger stimulants."[15]

A newspaper artist for the *World* drew an original rendition of Helga and Clara wearing their reformed costumes and toting knives and guns. The caption read: "Mrs. Estby and Her Daughter Walked Armed from Spokane," and it was signed J.C. Fineman. Then one brief sentence gave the ominous news that had shattered the trust, dreams, and determination of a mother and daughter to rescue their family, crushing their earlier exhilaration. Evidently, they discovered on Christmas Eve afternoon that the mysterious sponsor refused to honor the contract. The *World* reported Helga's news: "The object of the long tramp was to make money, but the woman who engaged them to do it has gone back on her contract."[16]

The sponsor not only refused to honor the contract but also refused to provide train money to return home, a tragic omission that ultimately shaped the destiny of the Estby family. Helga had put such faith in a stranger's promises. The reporter provided no information on the identity of the sponsor or the women's profound disappointment. Only Helga's concern was noted by the reporter: "She is wondering how they are going to get home."[17]

Stunned by this harsh betrayal, Helga and Clara spent Christmas Eve among a crowded city of strangers, so far away from the family they loved. Now destitute and homeless, did they still light a candle on this most silent of nights?

16 HEARTBREAK AT THE MICA CREEK HOMESTEAD

I have heard news that diphtheria is in my house.

—NEW YORK DAILY TRIBUNE
MAY 2, 1897

During the following spring, Helga and Clara faced the reality of being penniless women eking out a living in New York City. They needed to fend for themselves in a city teeming with other immigrants, trying to earn enough money to live while also saving for two return tickets home. Women generally earned only half the wages for similar work as men did at the turn of the century; their prospects for saving looked bleak.[1]

They moved to Brooklyn to look for work because it was a less expensive place to live than Manhattan. Helga, an excellent seamstress and housekeeper, might have found employment this way. The large immigrant population of Brooklyn, however, filled the newspapers with similar "work wanted" advertisements. Tens of thousands of immigrants came to New York, first from northern and western Europe and then, after 1890, also from southern and eastern European countries. Although women now entered the labor force in factories, most worked in "women's jobs," primarily in the garment shops, textile mills, hosiery plants, or food production area. Workers faced long hours, dismal working conditions, occupational hazards, and low pay. A sixty-hour, five-and-a-half-day week was commonplace. Highly skilled labor that required training, and provided higher wages, was reserved for men. For example, in breweries, men were brewers and young women were bottle washers; in bakeries, men were bakers and women were boxers or "cracker-packers"; even in the garment industry, men performed the most highly skilled work of cutting the fabric in waistmaking.[2] The low pay for women in temporary menial labor provided only for bare survival needs; saving enough for two cross-continental train tickets verged on the impossible.

Two topics that appeared continually in the Brooklyn newspapers in the winter of 1897 likely perked Helga's interest after her experiences in Wyoming and Colorado. The "woman question," particularly the issue of suffrage, often made front-page news in the Brooklyn *Standard Union*. Similar to her experiences in Manistee, Michigan, when she was sixteen, both sides argued vociferously. Helga now knew firsthand that some western women enjoyed this privilege, and her travels kindled her growing belief that women did not deserve to be treated as inferior.[3] As a reporter noted, "Both are satisfied in their own minds, at least, that man is not much the superior of women after all."[4]

Headlines in the Brooklyn *Standard Union* showed that citizens here faced the same threat that Helga did—losing their home to foreclosure. Even when the amount of taxes owed was small, she saw that the government and banks acted with impunity toward delinquent taxpayers. A front-page article on January 14 told of 101 parcels of lands and homes being auctioned off in six wards because the owners could not pay their 1894 taxes. Citizens owing the city $164 on a property valued at $5000 lost it all to someone bidding $3200. A lot valued at $300 was sold off for $250 although the woman owed only $14.58. City claims of delinquency as low as $12 were enough to justify the sales.[5] Learning of these heartless stories while living in limbo in New York, Helga knew that the next letter from Ole could announce that their foreclosure date was imminent. Helga and Clara earned their own living during the winter and spring of 1897. But no matter how hard they worked, they were unable to earn enough money to return. They felt trapped by economics, thousands of miles away from their family.

Back on the farm in Mica Creek, Ole faced a far greater heartbreak than the threat of losing their land.[6] In early April, their fifteen-year-old daughter, Bertha, came down with a sore throat. This news made parents nervous, especially after the epidemic of diphtheria in Spokane the summer before. Most victims lived in Spokane where Bertha had worked for a few months as a domestic to help earn money for the family.[7] The previous fall, their eldest son, seventeen-year-old Olaf, contracted diphtheria when he worked in Spokane. He spent time in a sanatorium outside the city to heal, and like many older children and adults, he recovered. Then he returned to their Mica Creek home.[8]

At moments like this, Ole wanted Helga home more than ever. The worrisome seven months had now stretched into a year. Helga's letters gave no indication of when she could afford two train tickets. Nor did he have any extra funds to send them. He barely earned enough for basic expenses to feed and clothe a growing family of seven children. Even now, he needed help from the older children who worked in the city of Spokane. When he rode the horse into Rockford or saw his neighbors, they no longer asked much about Helga because it was such an embarrass-ment. He had no answers to explain her Pollyanna belief in a mysterious, but obviously unworthy, spon-sor. If the sponsor refused to give her the $10,000, would not a decent human being at least loan her the money to come back home to her family? Earning her way across America had proved that she could work. If she did not have the expenses of rent and food in New York, she would be able to pay back a loan.

Ole knew the fear Helga harbored for diphtheria after the scare in Minnesota where they saw so many children die. After the Minnesota County Health Department held meetings and sent pamphlets home on how to best keep the contagion from spreading in a family, parents usually decided on a plan of action. If a child came down with diphtheria, the mother generally would be the nurse caretaker, which meant a father's task involved taking care of the other children in an outbuilding, keeping them warm and fed. This way the primary caretaker would not inadvertently pass the disease to the other children.

When the doctor confirmed Bertha's diphtheria diagnosis, Ole ordered the other children to stay in an outside shed. "We were so cold," recalled Ida.[9] He and their oldest son, Olaf, tried to take care of Bertha and the other children as best they could. Each day Bertha grew worse and as her throat was swelling, she lay prostrate on her bed, hardly responding to her father's frantic attempts to get her to eat or drink something. He sat by her bedside late into the night. Ole likely remembered another time while Helga was away from home. Ida insisted on planning a party for her sister Bertha's tenth birthday, so he rode the horse six miles into the general store in Rockford to get the soda Ida needed to bake a cake.[10] He enjoyed seeing Bertha's surprise and excitement when her friends all showed up to celebrate.

Ole felt his stark helplessness in preventing his daughter from choking to death. Nor could he be Helga to give her a mother's comfort. Always before when their children were ill, she had nursed them back to health.

In the 1890s, medical doctors observed that the mild or strong onset of the disease did not always indicate the future prognosis. An apparently mild case could lead to death in three to four days. Mortality rates during the 1890s from this disease ranged from forty to seventy-five percent, highest if it was a young child who contracted the most virulent form known as "black diphtheria."[11] If children were attacked with this virulent form, doctors advised parents that the best they could do was to provide some relief to ease the pain and make every effort to avoid contaminating the other children. Small doses of whiskey mixed with milk were recommended to relax the victim, but Ole probably could not afford that luxury in his home.

No neighbor dared to come to help the family because they risked bringing the dreaded diphtheria back into their own home. So, Ole tried in vain to comfort his daughter, and Olaf watched his little sister's dying hours in horror. When Bertha died the next day, on April 6, Ole walked out to within a few feet of the shed and had to yell the terrible news to her brothers and sisters. They broke into crying and wailing. Ole, known by all for his loving nature as a father, did not dare comfort them for he likely carried the contagious bacteria himself. Instead, he walked over to his workshop and began to make his beloved daughter a simple pine coffin.[12] Something in the familiarity of having a tool in his hand, and the unimaginable reality of using it to build his own child's casket, may have broken through his days of silent stoic duty.

The next day, Ole drove the horse wagon to the Mica cemetery alone and buried his daughter next to her younger brother, twelve-year-old Henry. Neighbors watched in sadness. The minister refused to come to the cemetery until after Ole had dug a deep grave, buried Bertha, and covered the coffin with dirt.[13] The dread of diphtheria robbed a family of receiving even the most elementary acts of decency and comfort, normally common in this close community. No nourishing food to help restore a shattered soul, no offer of childcare to ease a parent's grief, no housecleaning aid to free Ole to care for the children, nor any visit from the clergy to offer spiritual sustenance during grief could be provided. A quarantined home meant a home bereft of human connection.

Helga soon learned the devastating news of her daughter Bertha's death. After seeing how virulent diphtheria in Minnesota could kill all of a family's children in a matter of days, she became alarmed, anxious to get home to nurse and protect the children. This propelled Helga to ask for public aid for the first time in her life.[14] Three daily newspapers covered her and Clara's desperate visit to the office of the Charities Commission to ask the city of Brooklyn to pay their way to Spokane. Both women were described as "respectable and intelligent" in the newspaper article, and Helga told Commissioner Brutes that they had walked all the way from Spokane. Independent and resourceful, Helga was used to relying on her own resources and had never considered asking for public assistance. "We wouldn't ask for it now, but that I have received news that diphtheria is in my house and that my daughter Bertha is dead."[15]

Commissioner Brutes explained to Helga that it was impossible to grant such a request but offered to send them to the almshouses. "That's not what we want," said Mrs. Estby. "We want the money to return instantly to our home. We will pay you back every cent of it."[16] The Commissioner then advised them to go to the Bureau of Charities on Schermerhor Street. The *New York Daily Tribune* provided extensive details about their unpaid mortgage, the wager, and the trip, including Helga's latest optimistic scheme to solve their financial problems: "She intended to pay it off by selling a book written by herself and her daughter, describing their travels . . . . They said that on their return to Spokane they would deliver an illustrated lecture on their adventures." It concluded with the news that the Bureau of Charities was also unable to assist them.[17]

The *Sun*, a sensationalist "danger and doom" newspaper, headlined an article with "Walked Here from Spokane: Mrs. Estby Tells a Harrowing Tale of Eight Years of Tribulation." In reporting on her plea to the

Helga and Clara had their pictures taken again in New York at the Obermüller and Sons photography studio, perhaps with hopes of selling these to earn money for their trip home. Helga titled this The Pedestrians.

Courtesy Robert Mackintosh Family Collection.
Detail of this photograph on page 204.

MRS. H. ESTBY and DAUGTER.
walked from Spokane Wash. to N.Y. City 4600 Mils.
Obermüller & Son. opp. 5 th' Str near 4 th' Ave.
New=York.

city Commissioners of Charities to pay their way back to Spokane, it gave a litany of misfortunes Helga and Ole faced in the past years, including her accident and surgery, the family's inability to pay the mortgage, Ole's accidents, and children's illnesses. Although not all facts can be verified, what is apparent was Helga's sense of being besieged at this point. Known for her independence, determination, and innate confidence, these traits appeared to be waning. In shock and grief, she lamented, "Now my daughter Bertha is dead."[18] While searching desperately for funds to return, unbeknownst to Helga, even more sorrow was coming to her home.

Within days after Bertha became ill, Ole's fear that he had not protected the other children in time came true. Nine-year-old Johnny also complained of nausea, a fever, and sore throat. Rather than a mild beginning, Johnny immediately showed stronger diphtheria symptoms because he was younger and more vulnerable. Both tonsils became so swollen he had the "bull neck," a devastating warning to the doctor that the most lethal form of diphtheria had entered the Estby household. Now Olaf and Ole tried to nurse Johnny. Although older children like Olaf often recovered from diphtheria, the same disease could be fatal to younger children. Unseen germs often lingered for months in an environment, suddenly taking a new victim long after a family believed their sanitation efforts were sufficient. They did not dare try to comfort the other children, so fourteen-year-old Ida had to take care of William, Arthur, and three-year-old Lillian all by herself in the cold shed during the quarantine. They could not go to school, could not have their papa hold them, could not say good-bye to their cherished sister Bertha, and could not help with Johnny. They also lived with an invasive fear that one of them could be next.

Four days later, on April 10, Johnny died. Once again, Ole had to yell this terrible news to the children in the shed and listen to their wails of grief and fear. This time Olaf helped his father build the coffin, rode on the wagon to the Mica Creek cemetery, and dug the grave for his little brother alongside his sister Bertha's grave.[19] But when they returned home, they still dared not comfort the other children or let them back in the home until the county health officials arrived to disinfect the house. Ida cried to Ole that they were so cold in the shed, but he was afraid to give them extra blankets that might harbor the invisible killers. The family now had lost their third child within a year and a half. He listened to the complaints from the shed and prayed that no other child carried the bacteria that was destroying his family. As he crawled exhausted into bed, the heartbroken father must have wondered again if he had done enough to save his children. Did he give the right care? And he asked a question that remained until he was on his own deathbed, a question he knew his children also wondered: Would this have happened if Helga had been home?

17

HOMEWARD BOUND

For the first time in history this continent is traversed
on foot by women.... They crossed the borders of
fourteen commonwealths, dined with governors,
hobnobbed with railroad presidents, and saw the
sights of the continent and now are homeward bound.

—MINNEAPOLIS TRIBUNE
JUNE 2, 1897

While grieving the death of Bertha and fearful that diphtheria had entered their home, Helga learned that the city of Brooklyn refused to help, so she announced they would look for private funds. Helga's break came when famous New York railroad titan and after-dinner speaker Chauncy Depew was "greatly interested in the remarkable women" and "was touched" for a free railroad pass on his line to Chicago.[1] Helga probably personally solicited Depew's help. He also may have read about their plight in the newspapers. On May 4, almost one year since stepping out from Spokane, the women boarded a train in New York, bound for Chicago. From there, they walked to Minneapolis where they arrived on June 2 and stayed at the Scandia-Excelsior Hotel.[2]

This fortuitous stop drew the attention of interested news media and two lengthy articles appeared in the *Minneapolis Tribune* and *Minneapolis Times*. Reporters visited the women in their hotel where they were entertaining the kitchen staff with their adventures. In the month since Helga and Clara learned of Bertha's death and Helga made her plaintive plea for public assistance to return home, the mood of the mother and daughter had changed considerably. Before leaving New York, Helga evidently negotiated with the sponsor or sponsor's representative once more, attempting to get her book published. They left with an agreement that gave both Helga and Clara a strong sense of direction and satisfaction, even peace. After telling of their remarkable accomplishment and the failure to receive the wager, the *Minneapolis Tribune* mentioned that the matter was finally satisfactorily adjusted, and "the women will receive $10,000 when the book is written by them and describing their travels and adventures is completed."[3] The *Minneapolis Times* mentioned a similar settlement over the contract "between the two pedestrians and private parties in New York" adding that a book "will be published under the direction of the eastern parties."[4]

On their way home, Helga and Clara stopped in Minnesota where the Minnesota Times *and* Minnesota Tribune *carried extensive articles about their adventures.*

Courtesy Portch/Bahr Family Photograph Collection.
Detail of this photograph on page 216.

Anderson
EXTRA
FINISH
123 Washington Ave. S.
Minneapolis.

Part of the new agreement included funds for Clara to traverse by rail during the next summer on practically the same route over which she and her mother walked "for the purpose of securing illustrations for the book that is to be published." They seemed enthusiastic and trusting of these new arrangements.[5] These two lengthy June 1897 articles framed the scope of their historic achievement and set a tone suggesting how their "story" would be received by readers in America. After listening to Helga and Clara describe their adventures, both reporters used words such as "wonderful" and "marvelous" to summarize this 3500-mile transcontinental trek. After hearing Helga and Clara tell stories in the hotel, the *Minneapolis Times* recognized that the unique view of America these women experienced was comparable to best-selling British travel fables of the era. "A story was unfolded that would shine among the thrilling tales of Munchausen's adventures. This one was vastly superior, however, because true."

Then, in recognition of the rarity of such an effort, the *Minneapolis Times* writer mentioned that no women unattended had ever attempted this feat before. After detailing some of the narrow escapes from death the women encountered on the trip, the reporter concluded, "The incidents of the trip are certainly enough in quality and quantity to fill a good-sized volume."[6]

A description of the women in the *Minneapolis Tribune* used language that assured readers of the normalcy of the remarkable women who "presented a very home-like appearance" as they "modestly made themselves comfortable in the kitchen at the hotel, and were busy telling their story to the proprietor and waiters of the place." Interested in nineteen-year-old Clara, who "looks more like a maiden in some of the rural districts of Europe than an American girl," the reporter assures that "she appears in the vigor of health-budding womanhood." Helga is described as "of somewhat slender build, but has rosy cheeks."[7]

With the new contract arranged, the book plans made, and Helga and Clara homeward bound, they expressed excitement to soon be under their own roof in Washington State. Then they spoke of the value they placed on their experiences. Clara, who earlier admitted to being sick of the trip, now said she "considers that the trip is worth as much to her as a college course, for she has gained an extended knowledge of the country and has become adept in the reading of human nature."[8] Clara also expressed confidence that she could now handle rough situations when they arose. She usually carried the gun filled with insect powder and "brought it into play several times" when highwaymen and tramps attempted to accost her mother. She told how effectively the gun filled with red pepper worked: "a generous charge of the blinding pepper was as good as a whole police force."[9]

The newspapers stressed the women's mental abilities. "Both are women of high intellect and possess fine conversational powers .... and are enthusiastic over their work and adventures," noted the *Minneapolis Times* reporter. The *Times* also commented on the different political perspectives the mother and daughter held on the presidential candidates and free-silver election issues, recognizing their ability to think independently and disagree.[10] The *Minneapolis Tribune* reporter agreed, stating that both were apt talkers, and "although of Scandinavian birth, spoke the English language fluently and entertainingly."[11]

Declaring that "Mrs. Esby [*sic*] and Clara are the wife and daughter of a respectable Washington farmer," the *Times* added that the trip was partly planned for the health of Mrs. Estby, who "was threatened with consumption" and has now "regained entirely her fast failing health."[12] In no other newspaper was this reported. The women planned to remain in Minneapolis for a few days and then "endeavor in some manner" to secure train tickets home.

Helga evidently did not mention to the Minneapolis newspapers information on the death of her daughter Bertha or that diphtheria had invaded the home. It had been a month now since they had heard this disheartening news in Brooklyn. By this time, Helga and Clara may have come to some sense of peace, perhaps helped by the Norwegian Lutheran perspective on eternity. In this belief system, pastors often gave solace to grieving families that their beloved ones lived on in Heaven. Bertha's brief life belonged to God, and as a bereft mother and sister they likely found comfort in their church teachings that one day they would be reunited with their loved ones. Because they had been on the road with no reliable address, it is doubtful they knew of Johnny's death.

These two extensive articles conveyed the excitement the reporters felt about the value of Helga and Clara's upcoming book. Shorter newspaper articles had left much unsaid, especially concerning day-to-day life. Helga's book promised the possibility of a sweeping eyewitness record of American life in the great cities and unknown frontiers during the turbulent turn of the century. Stories showing their encounters with the humble and famous, including the nation's political leadership, could offer a glimpse into the fabric of American character. During an era where "the woman question" loomed large, Clara's differing ideas would add a fascinating generational viewpoint.

Their voices could also augment the male nature writers of the era in revealing how the grandeur and the harshness of the American landscape refreshed or intimidated them. And a book would offer insight into the emotional landscape of Helga, an articulate, complex, and intelligent immigrant woman living in an in-between era for women. Her own ideas about women's rights were clearly awakened as she encountered progressive women and men who insisted on reform in America. She may have found the solitude of the trip, especially after spending all her adult life caring for several children, a time of inner renewal, a sanctuary of silence. Although perhaps she longed only to be near her family each and every day that she walked farther away.

Her book could shed light into the mysterious sponsor of the trip, although it appears she never knew the exact identity of the wealthy New York woman who preferred "not to indulge her name."[13] Helga consistently stated that central to the sponsor's motivation was to prove the physical strength and endurance of women, and their ability to provide for themselves. For almost 3500 miles Helga and Clara had proved this splendidly. In light of the immense jeopardy in such a venture, it is conceivable the calculating sponsor never expected to have to pay up, and Helga and Clara arriving a few days late gave the unprepared sponsor a way out. A $10,000 wager is worth over $200,000 in 2002 dollars, a considerable gamble for the sponsor and presumes a person of exceptional wealth.[14] Clearly there appears to be a connection to the clothing industry that benefited from the women demonstrating the controversial short skirts. The *San Francisco Chronicle* indicated in the first announcement of the trip that the women "are under contract to a manufacturer of a health costume."[15] This same information came forth in another article stating, "Mrs. Estby and daughter will be paid a certain sum of money on their arrival in New York for their services in advertising the dress."[16] Two articles mention the

Weary Waggles that they wore, perhaps the name of a company that produced the bicycle skirts.

Helga consistently refers to her plans to write a book, but this appears to be her own idea, not the initial sponsor. An avid reader, perhaps she harbored a desire to become a writer. She mentions writing in her notebook daily, sending hundreds of pages home, and one article quotes her as saying "we write a complete account of the day's experiences and mail these immediately to the New York people who put up the wager. These daily letters will be published in book form at the conclusion of our trip."[17] If the original sponsors were primarily connected to the publishing world, however, nothing in Helga and Clara's late arrival altered the adventuresome transcontinental story. Their accomplishment offered living proof that women were a lot stronger than most people believed in the 1890s, a direct refutation to the lingering Victorian belief that physical exertion endangered women. It is unlikely a publisher would reject such a fascinating story on a technicality of arrival time. Most of their accounts spoke of publishing a book as an additional way to earn money beyond the wager.

The *New York World*, a progressive Pulitzer paper, was the first to announce their proposed trek in the April 26, 1896, newspaper under their "new women" column. Helga and Clara needed to go directly to the newspaper office on their arrival, so this newspaper likely served as a conduit for the mysterious sponsor. Newspapers at the turn of the twentieth century liked to draw attention to contests and wagers to interest readers. William Randolph Hearst, owner of the *New York Journal* and *San Francisco Examiner*, capitalizing on the bicycle craze in 1896, staged a San Francisco to New York cross-continental bicycle relay race during the same summer as Helga and Clara's walk. Much like riders of the Pony Express, the cyclists carried a news item across the nation in 13 days and 29 minutes.[18] What her book could tell readers is how she first heard of this wager and whether any Spokane connection existed, which was only mentioned in Indiana. All other articles refer to New York or eastern sponsors. The Spokane connection is unidentifiable, and if one did exist, it seems that a "wealthy suffragette" would have provided money for Helga and Clara to return on train to their family. She states that the wager "was arranged through the instrumentality of a friend in the East," a plausible explanation. A Spokane friend may have "conceived the idea" and helped make the connection with an eastern friend. But all this information has been lost.[19]

Exuberant to be homeward bound, and renewed by the strong press coverage they received in Minnesota, they now knew their distinctive accomplishment intrigued others. They looked to the future to write and illustrate the book, apparently confident they would finally receive the $10,000 to solve their family's difficulties. When they read the newspaper's glowing and thorough accounts of their adventure, they gathered copies of the articles to take home to show Ole and the children. These two treasured articles of their triumphant trip eventually became the only thin membrane of memory that kept this story alive.

18

LOST AND FOUND

Take care of this story, honey.

—HELGA TO GRANDDAUGHTER, THELMA

Helga and Clara returned to a husband and family overwhelmed by tragedy and filled with grief and hostility. "Johnny's dead too" were probably the first words Helga heard after arriving home.[1] She came back to Spokane more as a villain than a heroine. The memory of a cherished family life and home had motivated Helga to extraordinary efforts; it was what she longed to save. But after thirteen months of absence, the loving home she and Clara remembered no longer existed. Depending on when they arrived back, their home was probably still under quarantine. The children were not allowed to attend school or church, no one dared visit their infectious home, nor was Ole welcomed into other people's home after caring for his two dying children. The family suffered for weeks without comfort in their anguish.

Bertha's and Johnny's death did not just take the children, but became the breeding ground for anger, blame, and lifelong bitterness toward Helga for leaving.

She had flagrantly broken the most basic code of Victorian and Norwegian motherhood: mothers belong in the home. Helga heard the particular agonies of the children's dying days and saw her husband's heartbreak and sense of failure. She felt the bewilderment and resentment of the remaining children who spent such terrifying days alone in the cold shed. This all added to her deep grief and guilt. The weight of the unspoken question, "Would she have been able to save them?" was unanswerable, but also unlikely. And she carried the burden of knowing that she missed giving her children a mother's comfort in their dying days.

Helga left a husband and seven children at home for a year in pursuit of an inconceivable, dubious, and ultimately unsuccessful venture in an era when the belief in separate spheres for men and women still prevailed. Norwegians traditionally embraced a more rigid separation of men's and women's roles than even Americans, a pattern they brought as immigrants to a new land. In the "Little Norway" enclave of Mica Creek, disapproval was strong, which added to Ole's humiliation among his Scandinavian neighbors. "It wasn't looked upon well by the local farmers," recalled Nels Siverson. Even more telling was the moral reason he gave. "It wasn't the right thing to do."[2]

Perhaps even more galling to her Scandinavian neighbors was how her very act was a public admission of her husband's inability to provide and demonstrated a lack of submission to his authority or influence. She chose to direct her own destiny, to make up her own mind. An interview in the *Spokesman-Review* the day she left on the trip quoted Helga admitting, "It is easy to figure it out on paper, but it will be quite another thing to do as we have planned, but we have made up our minds as well as all arrangements."[3]

If criticism existed before she left, the crescendo against Helga's abandonment peaked when neighbors learned of the death of the children. This tragedy reinforced the mantra of motherhood that insisted a mother belonged in the home. Clergy, inspirational writers, and literature for and about women often espoused this viewpoint. "Woman was created to be a wife and a mother; that is her destiny.... She was born to be queen in her own household, and to make home cheerful, bright, and happy," expressed Orestes Brownson, a male social reformer of the era. "We do not believe women, unless we acknowledge individual exceptions, are fit to have their own head."[4]

When Helga ventured forth on this public walk away from home, she clearly saw herself as "fit to have her own head," to make up her own mind. Then Helga came home with nothing but additional flimsy promises from a sponsor whose word had already proved untrustworthy. When she returned to her isolated, grieving, and angry family, her own grief and guilt caused her "to have a sort of breakdown. She assumed a very different personality and withdrew into herself and kind-of lost her mind."[5] Helga had spent every day since she was sixteen years old bearing, nursing, nurturing, and raising children, and then she risked her life in a determined quest to save their family's home. It must have been unimaginable that her mother's heart could be questioned.

Helga and Clara did not write the book the next summer or give any illustrated lectures. Helga no longer wanted to present their adventures to the public, subjecting herself to more scathing disapproval. Beyond that, her walk across America became a taboo topic within the family. This family story was silenced, simply never talked about again. Ever.[6] It was as if their experiences could be erased from the family's history—a shameful act of a mother—never to be remembered. It is likely that the combination of Helga's own grief, the stinging criticism questioning her devotion as a mother, and the family's anger merged to erase the story. If it took silence to preserve the fragile bonds within her family, and restore friendships and respect within her cherished community, this was a cost she was willing to pay.[7]

What Helga imagined would be a tragedy, instead became a new start for the family. On a bleak day, March 28, 1901, the family's cherished farm was foreclosed and sold at a sheriff's sale.[8] The economy had improved by the time the Estbys moved back into Spokane, which allowed Ole to utilize his carpentry skills again. He entered into a successful contracting business with his son Arthur and eventually built the family an even finer two-story home on Mallon Street in another neighborhood where many Scandinavians lived. Clara attended a business college and began a lifelong career in the financial world.

Helga, a resilient woman, regained her emotional health. Although Helga came home to Spokane without an external prize, the walk across America gave her inner perspectives and resources that shaped the remaining half of her life in significant ways. If the circumstances of her life before the trip reinforced a more monolithic view on women, her broader experiences made this no longer possible. Not only was she exposed to ideas on America's "new woman," she and Clara were perceived as such by others. She had not only forged through swollen rivers and mountain passes, she had forged an identity that proved ordinary women could be physically strong, economically independent, and mentally tough.

Her travels across the continent also introduced her to crosscurrents of political attitudes toward women and awakened her belief that women deserved full citizenship, including the right to vote. Living back in

---

(following pages) The Estby family, around 1910, after they had moved back to Spokane and Ole had established a successful contracting business. Ida, Arthur, William, Lillian are in the back; Ole and Helga in the front. Clara is absent. By then five children had passed away.

Courtesy Portch/Bahr Family Photograph Collection.
Detail of this photograph on page 228.

the city, she became actively involved in the nation's suffrage movement by attending meetings and marching in the city suffrage demonstrations.

After her walk across America, she no longer sought all her satisfaction within her private sphere but instead gave her energy to issues in public life. This led to more friendships with a variety of women from many neighborhoods in Spokane.[9] She loved listening to the news on the radio, especially political programs, and kept an enduring interest in politics all her life. She believed her opinion as a citizen mattered. Helga regularly attended Spokane City Council meetings and voiced her perspective in public demonstrations. Those who knew her sensed her abiding and patriotic love for America, a permanent legacy enhanced by her encounters across the land in 1896.

Prior to her travels across the continent, her actions showed enormous confidence in one's individual effort and responsibility to solve problems. But her active interest in the compelling election issues of 1896, and personal encounters with Jacob Coxey, Mary Baird Bryan, and western populists introduced her to the need to work collectively on solving the nation's glaring problems. The humility of her destitution in Brooklyn taught her that sometimes individual effort alone was not enough in an unjust system. No matter how hard she and Clara worked in New York, with women's wages so low, she felt helplessly trapped. Once she returned to Spokane, she began to work with others on issues that concerned her. "The big issue at the time was suffrage for women," writes her great-great-granddaughter Darillyn Bahr. "Helga would march up and down with her . . . signs fighting for the right of women to vote."[10]

In 1913, Ole died from a fall off the roof of a house he was repairing. Sometime after his death, Helga set up a room of her own where she began learning to paint and finally started writing her memoirs of the trip across America. Helga's granddaughter, Thelma, and grandson, Roland, moved in with her in 1924 after the death of their father, Arthur. At this time, Helga's unmarried adult children, Ida and William, also lived with her. These were the happy days that Thelma remembered with her beloved grandma.

Helga's awakened curiosity about the world continued even after a leg injury from a taxicab accident in 1916 limited her movement for the rest of her life. She still loved to be on the go, and Thelma recalled how sometimes they would take the streetcar, ride to the end of the line out by Minnehaha Park, get out to walk around the beach and the woods, and then come back. "She just liked to see things."[11]

During these years, Helga secretly wrote hundreds of pages on yellow foolscap paper, finally describing their adventures across America. In the privacy of her upstairs room, she created a special space to write and draw. It was here that Helga told her granddaughter to "take care of this story," although the story remained a complete mystery to Thelma. No one ever told her that her grandmother walked across America.

One afternoon after Helga's death in 1942, Ida's younger sister Lillian came over to the house. While cleaning up, these two daughters of Helga lit a burn barrel in the backyard and tossed the hundreds of pages of their mother's manuscript into the fire. Perhaps they hoped the devouring flames would forever silence the story of their mother's actions that so shamed the Estby children. Ida's memories of caring for her frightened brothers and sisters in the cold shed scarred her life forever. "Ida never forgave her mother and always blamed her for the trip," recalled Thelma, "and neither did my father."[12]

While flames were destroying Helga's detailed memoirs, a daughter-in-law, Margaret, discovered the scrapbook with the two Minnesota news clippings of Helga and Clara's journey. She secretly took them. Margaret's husband, William, also still harbored resentment over his mother's journey, the death of his brother and sister, and the frightening cold days in the shed. So she did not even tell him of her discovery.[13]

But she knew Helga's story deserved to be saved. Twenty-six years later, after her husband's death in

Around sixty years of age, Helga enjoyed attending musical and cultural events in the city of Spokane, and she worked actively for the suffragette movement.

Courtesy Portch/Bahr Family Photograph Collection.

1968, Margaret finally passed on the news clippings to Helga's granddaughter, Thelma. She found out for the very first time what "story" her grandmother was writing. "I was amazed when I read the clippings because grandma never once mentioned the trip," recalled Thelma. "If Margaret hadn't saved these, the story would have been lost forever."[14] So silent had been this family story for over seventy years that Norma Lee, her other granddaughter, also had never heard of her grandmother's adventures.[15] "That's history they destroyed!" lamented Helga's grandson, Roland. "They never even asked if others of us in the family might want these."[16] He also had never heard that his grandmother had taken this trip even though he lived with her.

When Thelma heard the wonder of what her grandmother had accomplished, she took to heart Helga's charge, given to her forty-four years earlier when she was a young child, "to take care of this story." Now a mother and grandmother herself, Thelma vowed to fulfill her grandmother's request to keep this once-silenced story alive.

No longer would shame, silence, or neglect prevent the Estby grandchildren from knowing their own distinctive heritage. Thelma became the storyteller and began the tradition of keeping this grand history alive in her family to pass on to the next generation. Thelma's granddaughter, Darillyn Bahr, found her great-great-grandmother a source of inspiration when exploring her story for a school research paper. "She was one woman who kept on growing as a human being and never stopped."[17] It was Thelma's eighth-grade grandson, Doug Bahr, who entered the Washington State History Day Contest with his story "Grandma Walks from Coast to Coast." After telling what he knew about his great-great-grandma from the two Minnesota articles and oral family history, the fourteen year old concluded with a young person's instinctual understanding of why family memory and story matter. "I do not know if this story matters to others outside the family," he writes. "But no matter what adventures the future may bring for me, I know I can always count upon the determination, courage, and talent that is part of my heritage."[18]

Doug does indeed use these skills that are a part of his heritage. In his early thirties in 2002, Doug works as a firefighter and emergency medical technician in a suburb of Seattle. As part of a first-response team to fires, traumatic car accidents, suicides, drug overdoses, and deaths in the home, he needs to stay calm and level headed, use his analytical skills to think quickly, and recognize and adapt to problems in a proactive way. He still remembers his feelings while learning about the self-reliance, courage, and adventuresome spirit of his great-great-grandmother.

Helga's story *does* matter, and because this family became story keepers, her walk across America can now endure in the growing legacy of once-forgotten vibrant women in American life.

A Reflection on the Silencing of Family Stories

All families tell stories that are repeated to the next generation; sometimes stories even develop mythic qualities. Folklorists, anthropologists, sociologists, and psychologists have long seen the importance of family stories in shaping how we sense ourselves and our place in the world. "All of us, long after we've left our original families, keep at least some of these stories with us, and they continue to matter, but sometimes in new ways," claims Elizabeth Stone, author of *Black Sheep and Kissing Cousins: How Our Family Stories Shape Us.* "At moments of major life transitions, we may claim certain of our stories, take them over, shape them, reshape them, put our own stamp on them, make them part of us instead of making ourselves part of them. We are always in conversation with them, one way or another."[1]

Yet personal, family, and cultural forces contributed to the almost total silencing of Helga's stunning story. Helga's written memoirs of her journey, if read to the following generations of her large family, would have offered a rich reservoir of stories for her grandchildren. But the family united in their communal silencing of

243

this chapter in their mother's story. Even Helga's grandchildren who lived in her home had never heard of her achievement. Helga chose not to tell her grandchildren any stories of her adventuresome trip, and then her daughters burned her written manuscript.

In reality, all kinds of family stories are silenced. Common examples include those surrounding origins of birth, illness, and causes of death, such as, adoption, out-of-wedlock births, parentage, abortion, depression, mental illness, or suicide. Such silencing is often a combination of unspoken internal and external sanctions. These sometimes happen consciously, such as when persons are trying to protect a family's image in the face of alcoholism, family violence, eating disorders, sexual abuse, or origins of birth and death. However, at times the silencing of such stories affect those who need to hear them to correctly interpret events in their own lives. For example, a sixty-year-old physicist, who believes her brother was irrevocably damaged by their father's treatment of him, observed, "Some of that damage might have been mitigated if my brother could understand what had happened to my father to make him behave in those ways."[2] Family stories are silenced when strong pressures converge to deny a real experience.

But far more common are the stories that stay silent through neglect. For example, until quite recently, the voices of ordinary men and women were seldom published or included in academic study.[3] When a culture devalues one's story, so do individuals. Fortunately, exceptions exist, such as the women who chronicled their wagon trips to the west and passed their diaries on to family members who kept these stories alive in the family.

But, more often, silencing happens unconsciously and unintentionally when we "fail to notice that we fail to notice." Six common threads intertwined to contribute to the silencing of Helga's story for so many years. Any one of these can be sufficient cause to silence family stories.

BREAKING A CODE

In Helga's situation, she broke the central code of her culture, in this case that "mothers belong in the home." This code was particularly strong in Norwegian-American communities, church communities, and the Victorian culture that then prevailed in America. Few married women even worked outside the home, an action that many considered unladylike, even "immoral," especially when a husband and children needed them. Helga not only left seven children at home, but one was even a toddler who had recently turned two years old. As expressed by Martin Siverson, Ole's best friend in their Mica Creek community, "It wasn't right to do." This code was deeply rooted in Helga's life experience. Given that "a mother's place is in the home" had been her own value for twenty years, she was vulnerable to feelings of self-censure for leaving.

For years Helga had contributed to the silence surrounding Clara's birth by apparently falsifying
Clara's birth date. During her pregnancy with Clara,
she broke two 1890s codes: that women should be
married before giving birth, and, if pregnant out of
wedlock, they should marry the father of the child.
Helga and Ole's choice not to tell Clara about her true
birth father probably began in their desire to protect
her. However, they underestimated the value of this
information to Clara and the impact on Clara when
she learned of this deception in her adult years from
parents she once trusted. By the time the women
arrived in New York, Clara evidently had learned the
truth about her birth and told a reporter "she was
born in Michigan," not on the Minnesota prairie after
her mother's marriage. She became estranged from
her family during her early adult years and changed
her last name to Doré, a name her family believes
might be her biological father's name. She later rec-
onciled with the family.

UNDERESTIMATING THE WORTH

Another primary thread of silencing occurs when others underestimate the value of a person's experiences.
This is "negation by neglect," and it reigns as the
dominant cause for the loss of family stories. Either
the worth of the experience or even the worth of the
person is underestimated. But Ida and Lillian never
could have known the worth of their mother's mem-

oir. In Helga's situation, the family had no idea that her written story would offer a significant contribution to American history. This makes sense considering that historians during her lifetime did not value the stories of ordinary women. More surprising was that her immediate family did not consider Helga's story a positive resource for future generations.

The burning of her manuscript recalls how close the writings of others, such as African-American author Zora Neal Hurston, came to being destroyed. Destitute and no longer acclaimed in her old age, Hurston was considered of "little worth" at her death. When county workers came to clean out her house, they started to burn the clutter. One recalled that Zora was once a respected writer and, hoping there might be something of worth to augment county expenses, hosed down the fire just in time to recover her charred papers.[4] It took more than fifty years and a seismic shift in appreciating the worth of African-American women writers before her acclaimed book, *Their Eyes Were Watching God*, was republished. Her writings proved pivotal for inspiring the next generation of African-American women writers, such as Alice Walker. Only recently, with the growing publications of multicultural stories available in schools and libraries, are all children in America able to read about the lives of others with their same ethnic heritage.

BELIEVING ONE'S STORY IS INCOMPREHENSIBLE

When an experience seems incomprehensible to others, it can contribute to the silencing of stories. None of Helga's neighbors could imagine what she encountered because such an endeavor existed outside their own knowledge. For women to walk unescorted in the wilderness, to sleep unprotected in railroad station houses or in strangers' homes, to wander alone in New York, Chicago, Denver, Omaha, and Salt Lake City, and to meet with powerful political leaders was simply incomprehensible to her immigrant neighbors. Even the freedom of movement Helga knew from wearing the new bicycle skirts was something the women in Mica Creek could not imagine.

Helga had no one to talk with about nonconformist ideas concerning the possibilities for women or the injustice of entrenched roles. Although women neighbors could imagine a pregnancy before wedlock, in Norwegian communities it was far less understandable that a woman did not marry the man who was the father of the child. Helga's conversations along the rural and urban routes of 1896 America meant she inevitably experienced the loosening of boundaries that characterized the turn of the century. "Something happens at the end of a century," wrote one historian referring to the 1890s. "Rules are altered, boundaries are breached, and fundamental attitudes are changed."[5] Helga's lost stories of encounters with American citizens could have shed light on this theory in lively ways.

Other experiences that often seem beyond comprehension to family members and therefore remain unheard involve war memories, early poverty, sexual identity, academic, work, and professional life. Some of the first generation of educated persons within a family speak of similar separation and silencing that occurs as they advance beyond their parent's educational level. The experiential gaps that emerge contribute to silences within families, an unspoken acknowledgment that each other's experiences are simply beyond understanding.

SEALING THE SHAME

Stories that family members perceive as shameful often stay silenced. Shame involves a painful feeling of having lost the respect of others, even if this is culturally bound. This can be caused by "perceptions of improper behavior or incompetence which brings dishonor or disgrace to oneself or one's family, something perceived as regrettable, outrageous, or unfortunate."[6] Sealing the shame often surrounds stories of incest, alcoholism, mental illness, violence against women during wartime, or AIDS. Shame can include a deep feeling about oneself over something that seems unchangeable.[7] Helga could not change the fact that she left home and that two children died, a regrettable, unfortunate, and some say, outrageous act. In her mind, she embarked on this walk as an act of love for her family; she was determined to try to save their family home by this unique opportunity that presented itself during the spring of 1896. Yet, after returning home, she knew her husband and children felt shame because her leaving home had brought dishonor and disgrace to the family, especially after the two children died. Given these perceptions and her own, Helga likely decided the less said about her actions, the better. The act of burning the manuscript may have been her daughters' effort to seal forever the shame of their mother's aberrant actions.

Pretending that Clara was Ole's child sealed the shame of her out-of-wedlock pregnancy. She had practiced silence before, and she could do it again. To go public with her story after the children's death would place her actions under far more severe scrutiny than her initial trip. Victorian values still prevailed, and she would not want to add more pain to her family. Her life demonstrated that she valued her close connections within the Norwegian-American community. Current researchers on the psychology of women "all agree that interpersonal intimacy is the profound organizer of female experience."[8] The importance that women place on the establishment and maintenance of close relationships clearly characterized Helga's life, too.

Every country needs individuals who refuse to be silenced when breaking out of unhealthy cultural norms, despite the criticism. This courageous spirit allowed Hildegard of Bingen to ignore criticism when she left a male monastery and established a highly influential female monastery in twelfth-century Europe; led Jane Addams to break the lifestyle norms for privileged educated females by moving to the inner city of Chicago to establish Hull House and live among the poor; and inspired Martin Luther King Jr. to defy segregation laws and lead a nation in civil disobedience protests even after his home was bombed. Each of these leaders influenced their societies to make important innovative changes, but their success depended on ordinary women and men speaking up and risking criticism. Once convinced that women deserved to be full voting citizens, Helga stayed actively committed to the suffrage movement, undeterred by disapproval.

KEEPING THE PEACE

A family story that threatens internal relationships will be silenced by those wanting to maintain fragile family bonds. This is particularly true of women who self-silence.[9] In the Victorian home, women were expected to create a supportive climate for domestic life, helping all family members to get along.[10] There was such bitterness toward Helga, mingled with deep grief and hurt, that avoidance of any discussion of their walk across America must have been their way to cope and maintain the family relationships. If Helga did not speak about her trip, she could avoid personal hurt and the problems it raised in the family.[11]

Her approach represents a common pattern for handling unpleasant facts, especially family stories that can be hurtful. In *Vital Lies, Simple Truths*, in the chapter called "What You Don't See Won't Hurt You," Daniel

Goleman describes how a "semblance of cozy calm can be maintained by an unspoken agreement to deny the pertinent facts." When describing how families and groups deny information that makes them uneasy, he states, "We tune out, we turn away, we avoid. Finally we forget, and forget we have forgotten . . . . It is easier to go along with the silent agreements that keep unpleasant facts quiet and make it hard to rock the boat."[12]

Often families consider whether all truths should be told and recognize that the balance between "shedding veils and shielding painful truths" is a subtle one. Clearly there are times when a family or individual may wisely choose that a story needs to be private. "Every family has secrets," claims psychologist J. Bradshaw. "Some are benign and constructive, protecting the family and/or an individual member and aiding their growth and individuality. Others are toxic and destructive, destroying trust, freedom, intimacy, growth, and love."[13] Keeping Clara ignorant of her biological father kept Ole and the other children from hearing more about Helga's pregnancy by another man, a truth Helga believed should not be told.

Helga's decisions were not unusual for the late Victorian era. "If we don't talk about it, it will go away," was one way in which pain and grief were handled. In the mid-1800s, there was a significant amount of sentimentality and religious literature surrounding grief and mourning over the death of children. These included consolation literature emphasizing the afterlife as joyous and available to all believers. This was aimed primarily at women, who were considered especially prone to grieving because of their focus on motherhood and expressiveness.[14] Poems and stories about death (particularly a mother's bereavement) had been standard fare in the middle-class women's magazines, until they abruptly stopped in 1875 when Helga was fifteen. Victorian values may have caused this shift. As one woman of the era explained, "A woman's highest duty is so often to suffer and be still."[15] For the next one hundred years, during the rest of Helga's life, death and grieving became a taboo topic in the United States and no articles appeared in any of the six major women's magazines.[16] It was common behavior to keep painful experiences inside. Helga's granddaughter Thelma mentioned that she never heard Helga talk about her husband after his death, nor does anyone in the family know much about her son's death right before she left on the walk across America, or the death of Ole and Helga's first-born son in Minnesota.

After Ole's death, Helga did choose to write her memoirs in great detail. Hundreds and hundreds of pages came forth, but still she kept them secret from the sons and daughters, knowing they harbored anger. Yet the comment to her granddaughter Thelma to "take care of this story for me" suggests she held hopes that someday her story could be told. Her very act of creation indicates that she was validating the worth of her experiences, at least to herself. Her need to remember and share her life story remained.

The children's anger over Helga's actions remained until their death. By staying silent, Helga avoided the continuous expressions of her children's resentment. "She was never forgiven for leaving" was repeated often by family members, although they took very loving care of their mother in her elder years.[17] The Victorian emotional culture gave little room for the expression of anger by women or children in the family. Anger was perceived as particularly menacing to family life. Prescriptive literature had firm advice on domestic discord and marital quarrels. Prohibitions existed against angry displays by children against parents. The overarching belief was that the family must be preserved against emotional storms.[18]

The fragility of the family after Helga returned was obvious to each member. They still were in dire economic circumstances and emotionally broken. It was likely they kept silent partly as a way to contain their anger. During Helga's later years, when she enjoyed talking about politics, her family always "shut her up," and her granddaughter said she seldom spoke back. This repression may be how she handled her own anger at being silenced

Helga Estby, bilingual since childhood, always loved reading a good book. During later years she wrote a memoir of her cross-continent adventures. Circa 1930s.

Courtesy Portch/Bahr Family Photograph Collection.
Detail of this photograph on page 242.

for expressing her unpopular political views. Helga un-doubtedly harbored some anger at the unknown wealthy New York woman and collaborating sponsors, if any, for their choices. She endured the humiliation of coming home empty-handed, susceptible to the charges that she had been a fool to trust a stranger's wager. The family also spoke of Helga's change to a more melancholy per-sonality after the trip. Although she did not live in a deep depression from the silencing of the self, she lost some of the exuberance within her family that they say used to exist. But she continued to express a vibrant interest in life, friendships, politics, culture, hobbies, and her family.

Because of the ways Helga's story was silenced, whether from internal or external censure, her family never knew or valued the fullness of their mother's life. However, even the family silencing failed to daunt her ongoing interest in the world around her, whether in marching for women's rights, attending the theater, or joining the Sons of Norway. Nor did this stop her per-sonal growth and desire to write her story, although she wrote it secretly. "Censorship silences," states Tillie Olsen in her groundbreaking book *Silences* where she addresses the circumstances that often stifled acts of creation. She explores unnatural silencing, the thwart-ing of something that is struggling to come into being. "Where the gifted among women (and men) have remained mute, or have never attained full capacity, it is because of circumstances, inner or outer, which oppose the needs of creation."[19]

The Importance of Story Keeping

The six threads that contributed to muting this gifted woman's story often surround the silencing of many family stories. For both internal and external reasons, Helga's story was thwarted as she struggled to bring it into being. Helga's adventurous and life-shaping journey was not a tragedy. But the loss of her story, destroyed forever with the flick of a match, is a great misfortune, not only for her family but for all persons interested in understanding more of American life during a significant transitional time in history. Helga must have experienced bittersweet memories as she composed her memoirs. How exciting it would be to read this original manuscript, to see through her lively intellect and courageous spirit the American life she and Clara encountered along their way. The silencing of this walk through the social, cultural, economic, and political as well as geographic landscape of late-nineteenth-century America means our country lost a sweeping eyewitness account of two women's encounters with the humble and the famous amid the burgeoning cities and frontiers.

Although Helga never received the $10,000, walking across America infused her life with significant intangible rewards. Throughout the newspaper accounts, Helga conveyed to reporters a quiet confidence that their goal was possible, that they expected to be able to achieve what everyone else told her was impossible. She exuded the positive attitude, boldness, and courage that often characterizes leaders. Yet, she admits to discouragement after the grueling walk through the long distances, mountains, and deserts of Idaho, Wyoming, and Utah. She overcame the discouragement, exhaustion, and criticism for stepping beyond her cultural norm, enjoyed and learned from much of what she encountered. By putting feet to her faith that "all things are possible with God," their arrival in New York confirmed this belief that was instilled during her childhood. According to her family, this vital faith proved to be a bedrock of strength, keeping her positively involved with life even while enduring the profound losses of six children, her husband, their beloved Mica Creek home, and her health before her death at eighty-one years old.

She also gained a lifelong love for America and appreciation for the kindness of the average men and women who live in this land. As she traveled the rails, Helga recognized the exaggeration of fears people held toward the unknown. She discovered the need to face down blind stereotypes and prejudices that limit individuals and the nation, whether her own earlier attitudes toward Native Americans and hoboes, or the cultural bias underestimating women's physical and mental strength. Helga recognized the strength she and Clara possessed as they forged their way across the land; this heightened her awareness of what women could do. Beyond individual efforts, though, she saw the essential force of communal strength. Walking though Colorado and Wyoming, where women had won the right to vote, and through America during the election fervor of 1896, awakened Helga to the possibilities for significant political change when people unite together. Ideas matter, as do cultural norms and legal structures, affecting both individuals and the nation she loved. This freed her to become actively involved in the suffrage movement, even when her daughters disapproved, and to believe that this nation should and would open full citizenship to women. Her grandchildren missed a rich vein of wisdom when they did not get to hear how she approached life's challenges, and her active belief in what can be called the art of the possible.

The gathering and sharing of the rag-rug remnants of our family's lives gives a gift to the next generation, a community of memory in a highly mobile world. Through developing written and oral histories, creating scrapbooks, telling stories around a dining table or campfire, displaying photographs and making videos, every family can weave an enduring rug of memories. Capturing the hopes, challenges, actions, disappointments, successes, pains, and joys inherent in every family gives children roots and wings. Other cultures practice the art of storytelling. In the Masai tribe in Kenya, for example, when a person dies, the greatest gift one can give a grieving person is to come and tell a story from the loved one's life. A collage of memories grow, giving the heart solace and healing, and the stories go on for generations. Remembering the past, telling the children the stories of parents and grandparents lives, can prove to be a pivotal resource in a young person's life, as Doug Bahr recognized in remembering his great-great-grandmother, Helga.

My hope is that Helga's story, once shrouded in silence, now can be linked with other voices to contribute to a fuller American history and to contribute to a growing dialogue on the causes and costs of silencing the story of a life.

Notes

INTRODUCTION

1. Thelma Portch, first interview by author, Almira, Wash., 1984.

2. Ibid.

3. M. Cummings, *The Lamplighter* (1854; reprint, New Brunswick, N.J.: Rutgers University Press, 1988), 6:104.

4. Thelma Portch, second interview by author, Almira, Wash., 1986.

5. Darillyn Bahr, "Coast to Coast," School Research Report, Wilbur, Wash., 1977.

6. T. Portch, second interview.

7. T. Portch, first interview.

8. Ibid.

1 | ON FOOT TO NEW YORK

1. "Tramp to New York," *Spokane* (Wash.) *Daily Chronicle*, May 4, 1896, p. 2.

2. Ibid.

3. "Coast to Coast," *Minneapolis Times*, June 2, 1897, p. 5.

4. "On a Long Walk," *Idaho Daily Statesman*, June 5, 1896, p. 3.

5. Ibid.

6. Letters from the Thelma Portch Collection. These include 1893 letters to Helga from her children, some undated letters and notes, and notes from Helga giving the date of Henry's death.

7. "Are Walking for Wages," *Walla Walla Union*, May 17, 1896, p. 4.

8. Nels Siverson, neighbor of the Estbys at Mica Creek, oral interviews, 1986, 1993. Nels' father, Martin Siverson, was Ole's best friend. Nels had been told the story by his father who had watched them start their walk from Mica Creek.

9. "Are Walking for Wages," *Walla Walla Union*, p. 4; "Two Women's Long Tramp," *New York Herald*, December 23, 1896, p.10; "From Spokane to New York: Two Women Tramps," *Lebanon Daily News*, December 19, 1896, p. 1.

10. "Women Walkers," *Minneapolis Tribune*, June 2, 1897, p. 4.

11. "The Story They Told," *San Francisco Examiner*, December 23, 1896, p. 4; "A Long Journey," *Fort Wayne Gazette*, November 19, 1896, p. 1; "Women Walkers Reach Plymouth," *Plymouth Republic*, November 19, 1896, p. 6.

12. "Women Pedestrians," *Daily Sun Leader*, August 27, 1896, p. 4.

13. "The Estbys Reach New York," *Spokesman-Review*, December 24, 1896, p. 2.

2 | MOTHERHOOD ON A MINNESOTA PRAIRIE

1. Ida Estby, daughter of Helga and Ole, Oral History at Cheney Cowles Museum, Spokane, Wash., 1973. Ida was a young girl when she watched the great Spokane fire destroy the heart of the business district in 1889. Because of this, she was included in a collection of transcribed oral interviews. The material provided valuable information on the Estby family far beyond her observation of the fire.

2. "History of Manistee County," (Minneapolis: Minnesota Historical Society files, 1996), 8.

3. Ida Estby, oral history interview.

4. Doug Bahr, "Grandma Walks from Coast to Coast," Eighth grade Essay, Almira, Wash., 1984. Not until after the walk across America, did the fact that Ole was not Clara's father become well known throughout the family. In her twenties, Clara formally changed her last name from Estby to Doré, which led to speculation from family members that this might be the name of her biological father. Her stated reason for the change was for "business purposes."

5.   Census Records, Minnesota, 1880; Doug Bahr, "Grandma Walks"; T. Portch, interviews. During Clara's childhood, Helga listed her birth as November 26, 1877, in census and family records, making her look like a legitimate child of her marriage with Ole.

6.   J.D. Holmquist, ed., *They Chose Minnesota: A Survey of the State's Ethnic Groups* (St. Paul, Minn., 1981), 221. In July of 1877, the government granted land patents to Ole and sixty-four mostly Scandinavian settlers, including two women, on fertile lands near the tributaries of the Lac qui Parle River in western Minnesota.

7.   Thelma Portch, first interview by author Almira, Wash., 1984.

8.   Thelma Portch, second interview by author, Almira, Wash., 1986.

9.   D. Bahr, "Grandma Walks."

10. Thelma Portch, family artifacts, Helga Estby notebook.

11. Ida Estby, oral interview.

12. Willa Cather, *My Ántonia* (Boston: Houghton Mifflin Company, 1918), 342.

13. M.S. Brinkman and W.T. Morgan, *Light from the Hearth: Central Minnesota Pioneers and Early Architecture* (St. Cloud, Minn.: North Star Press, 1982), 14.

14. C.D. Ruud, "Beret and the Prairie in Giants of the Earth," *Norwegian American Studies* 28 (1975), 217–245.

3 | The Crucible Years

1.   J. Narvestad, *The History of Yellow Medicine County* (Granite Falls, Minn.: Yellow Medicine County Historical Society, 1972).

2.   A. P. Rose, *An Illustrated History of Yellow Medicine County, Minnesota* (Marshall, Minn.: Northern History Publishing Company, 1914), 123.

3.   G.O. Sandro, *The Immigrant Trek* (Minn.: Self-Published, 1929), 44.

4.   J. Narvestad, *The History of Yellow Medicine County*.

5.   M.S. Brinkman and A.W. Morgan, *Light from the Hearth: Central Minnesota Pioneers and Early Architecture* (St. Cloud, Minn.: North Star Press, 1982), 18.

6.   L.G. Davis, *A Diphtheria Epidemic in the Early Eighties* (Sleepy Eye, Minn.: Minnesota Medical Report, 1934), 435.

7.   *Circular No. 1*, Minnesota State Board of Health, 1880.

8.   Ibid., 5.

9.   Ibid., 7.

10.   Yellow Medicine County 1887 Court Records, Homestead sales.

11.   Thelma Portch, second interview by author, Almira, Wash., 1986.

12.   R.P. Herriges, *Fire on the Prairie: Memories of Lac Qui Parle* (Madison, Minn.: The Heritage Press, 1980), 37.

13.   "Black Friday," *Canby News*, May 15, 1885, 4.

14.   "Minnesota Storm Damage," *Canby News*, June 24, 1885, 1.

15.   T. Portch, second interview.

16.   *Settler's Guide* (Spokane Falls, Wash., 1885), 56.

17.   Ibid.

18.   Thelma Portch, family artifacts. Helga kept both an advertisement for carpenters and an advertisement for "Residence Lots Cheap" from the *Spokane Falls Evening Chronicle* of September 21, 1886, in a scrapbook of memorabilia.

19.   J. Rasmussen, *New Land, New Lives: Scandinavian Immigrants to the Pacific Northwest* (Northfield, Minn.: Norwegian-American Historical Association, 1963), 7.

20.   *Spokane City Directory*, 1888.

4 | SUPRISES IN SPOKANE FALLS

1.   *Spokane Falls, Washington Territory: The Metropolis of Eastern Washington and Northern Idaho 1889* (Spokane, Wash.: Union Pacific Railroad, 1889), 6.

2.   "Spokane Tribe History," http://www.wellpinit.wednet.edu/spokan/history/timeline.php [November 3, 2001].

3. Ida Estby, daughter of Helga and Ole, Oral History at Cheney Cowles Museum, Spokane, Wash., 1973.

4. Darillyn Bahr, "Coast to Coast," School Research Report, Wilbur, Wash., 1977.

5. J. Fahey, *The Inland Empire: Unfolding years, 1879–1929* (University of Washington Press, 1986).

6. J. Rettman, "Prostitution in Spokane, WA: 1889–1908," (master's thesis, Eastern Washington University, 1994).

7. Spokane County Court Records, Lawsuits: 1890–1920.

8. "Lawsuit announcement," *Spokesman-Review*, September 23, 1888.

9. A. Trodd, *Domestic Crime in the Victorian Novel* (New York: St. Martin's Press, 1989).

10. Spokane County Court Records, Lawsuits, 1916. Helga was involved in a second lawsuit in 1916 that required her to elaborate on her first lawsuit against the city after a taxicab accident left her with permanent injuries. This provides rich information on the accident on Riverside Avenue during 1888.

11. Ibid.

12. Spokane County Court Records, 1889; Arlene Coulson "Research notes on Helga Estby's Family," Whitworth College History Project, 1986.

13. "The Jury in the Estley [*sic*] Suit," *Spokane Falls Review*, February 21, 1889, p. 4.

14. Spokane County Court Records, Mortgage Book, 1889.

15. Spokane County Court Records, Lawsuits, 1890.

16. Ida Estby, oral history interview, 1973.

17. Ibid.

18. Spokane County Court Records, Lawsuits, 1916.

1. C. Schwantes, "Spokane and the Wageworkers' Frontier: A Labor History to World War I," in *Spokane and the Inland Empire: An Interior Pacific Northwest Anthology*, ed. D. Stratton (Pullman, Wash.: Washington State University Press, 1991), 125.

2. E.T. Becher, *Spokane Corona: Eras and Empires* (Spokane, Wash.: Self-Published, 1974).

3. J. Rettman, "Prostitution in Spokane, Washington: 1889–1908" (master's thesis, Eastern Washington University, 1994).

4. Ibid.

5. "Call Grand Jury," *Spokesman-Review*, December 11, 1903, p. 1.

6. Ida Estby, daughter of Helga and Ole, Oral History at Cheney Cowles Museum, Spokane, Wash., 1973.

7. Ibid.

8. Ibid.

9. Spokane County Court Records, Mortgage Book, 1892.

10. Donna Miscovitch, notes from an interview with ninety-six year-old Amy Fundin who grew up on the Estby land after they lost the farm. Atwater, Calif., 1995.

11. Ida Estby, oral history interview.

12. Women's Club Authors, *Down Memory Lane* (Mica Community Publication, 1979).

13. "Walked Here from Spokane," *Sun*, May 2, 1897, p. 1.

14. Ida Estby, oral history interview.

6 | FINANCIAL FEARS AND A FAMILY DEATH

1. Letters from the Thelma Portch Collection. The letters from her children, some dated in 1893 and sent to Wisconsin, were treasured by Helga all of her life. Some are undated and without a postal address and could have been sent during the time when she walked for four hundred miles prior to 1896. No records in Wisconsin and Michigan have been

found confirming her parent's residence or death during these dates. Helga may have been visiting her family or a previous friend from Minnesota.

2. D. Stratton, ed., *Spokane and the Inland Empire* (Pullman, Wash.: Washington State University Press, 1991), 131.

3. Ibid.

4. Arlene Coulson, "Research notes on Helga Estby's family," Whitworth College History Project, 1986. The Spokane County Land Department records of mortgages and deeds include a series of Deeds and Loans that reflect this cycle of using loans to repay old debts; these are all included in "Mortgage Records," a series of books. On January 29, 1889, the Estbys borrowed $60 from H.L. Richardson on their Spokane Falls Saunders Addition 21, 22, 23 (Book T, p. 270) that was satisfied on October 28, 1889 (Book W, p. 467). On the day this was satisfied, Ole borrowed $250 from Adolph Munter against the same property; this was satisfied on June 14, 1890 (Book 13, p. 302). On the day this was satisfied, he borrowed $600 from H.L. Richardson against the same property; this was satisfied on April 23, 1891 (Book 13, p. 302). Four days later they took out a "Chattel Mortgage" with G.W. Frosh. Records only say "loan satisfied" (Book S, p. 129). On March 14, 1892, another "Chattel Mortgage" with J.E. Foster shows no record of this loan being satisfied (Book N, p. 524). However, on this same day, mortgage records show that they borrowed $700 from R. Livingstone, Trustee, Oregon Mortgage Company on the Lockwood (Mica) homestead, 160 acres (Book 41, p. 157); records only say "loan satisfied." Ten days later, on March 24, 1892, they borrowed another $235 from J.E. Foster on the Lockwood homestead (Book 33, p. 412); this loan was satisfied on July 2, 1894 (Book 33, p. 412). In the margin of this loan record is a note indicating Helga Estby was given power of attorney from Ole to sign. This may have been during the time he was injured and incapable of coming into the Spokane County Courthouse. Four days later, on July 6, they borrowed $1000 on their Lockwood homestead. This loan was never satisfied and was the source of their fear of losing their home and farm.

5. "Walked Here from Spokane," *Sun*, May 2, 1897, p. 1.

6. Letters from the Thelma Portch Collection.

7. Arlene Coulson, "Research Notes"; Doug Bahr, "Grandma Walks from Coast to Coast," Eighth-grade Essay, Wilbur, Wash., 1984. Family oral history includes mention of the death of the Estby's first son believed to be born in Minnesota and named Ole after his father.

8. A. Raaen, *Grass of the Earth: The Story of a Norwegian Immigrant Family in Dakota* (St. Paul Minnesota Historical Society Press, 1950), 80.

9. Thelma Portch, second interview by author, Almira, Wash., 1986.

7 | THE WAGER

1. "Women Globe Trotters," *Weekly Bedrock Democrat*, May 25, 1896, p. 1; "Walking for Pay," *Fort Wayne Sentinel*, November 18, 1896, p. 1.

2. "From Spokane to New York," *Deseret Evening News*, July 11, 1896, p. 5.

3. "Are Walking for Wages," *Walla Walla Union*, May 17, 1896, p. 4.

4. "Lives Wrecked by Wheeling," *Examiner*, July 1, 1896, p. 1.

5. Montgomery Ward & Co., Catalogue No. 57, Spring and Summer 1895, Unabridged Facsimile (New York: Dover Publications Co.).

6. "Women Globe Trotters," p. 1.

7. Ibid., p. 1.

8. See Patrick Geddes, a Scottish biologist, who wrote *The Evolution of Sex* in 1889 and argues for a typology of biologically determined sexual temperaments as a function of natural law.

9. Harvey Green, *The Light of the Home: An Intimate View of the Lives of Women in Victorian America* (Pantheon Books, 1983), 114.

10. Sheila M. Rothman, *Women's Proper Place* (New York: Basic Books, Inc., 1980), 24.

11. Ibid., 24.

12. Ibid., 34.

13. "From Spokane to New York: Two Women Tramps," *Lebanon Daily News*, December 19, 1896, p. 1; "Women Walkers Arrive," *New York Herald*, December 24, 1896, p. 7.

14. "Women of the Week," *World*, April 26, 1896, p. 24.

15. "Tramp to New York," *Daily Chronicle*, May 4, 1896, p. 2.

16. The 1896 *Spokane City Directory* lists Bertha as a domestic and Olaf as a gardener at the home of Isabel and Lewis Rutter, a prominent banker in town. It was common in Spokane for wealthy families to hire Scandinavian young people to work part-time in their homes. Clara may have also worked there to complete high school in the city. Both Bertha and Olaf returned to the homestead while Helga and Clara were still in New York in 1897.

17. "Tramp to New York," p. 2.

18. "Coast to Coast," *Minneapolis Times*, June 2, 1897, p. 5.

19. "Walk to New York," *Spokesman-Review*, May 5, 1896, p. 5.

20. "The Jury in the Estley [*sic*] Suit," *Spokane Falls Review*, February 21, 1889, p. 4.

21. "From Spokane to New York," p. 5.

22. H. Green, *The Light of the Home* (New York: Pantheon Books, 1983), 29.

23. Ibid., 57.

24. Nels Siverson, neighbor of the Estbys, interview, 1986.

25. *Spokane City Directory*, 1895.

26. "Are Walking for Wages," p. 4.

27. Thelma Portch, first interview by author, Almira, Wash., 1984.

1. Nels Siverson, neighbor of the Estbys at Mica Creek, oral interviews, 1986, 1993. Dr. L. Hustved, Secretary of the Norwegian-American Historical Association, St. Olaf College, Minnesota, interview, 1996. Dr. Hustvedt stated unequivocally that Helga's choice to leave home would ignite strong disapproval among their Norwegian neighbors. The belief that women belonged in the home was paramount in the 1890s among Norwegian families, nor should one "draw attention" to oneself as Helga needed to do to raise money along the route. Her actions would be considered "outrageous."

2. "Are Walking for Wages," *Walla Walla Union*, May 17, 1896, p. 4.

3. Ibid.

4. Ibid.

5. "Women Globe Trotters," *Weekly Bedrock Democrat*, May 25, 1896, p. 1.

6. "Umatilla Reservation and Its Inhabitants," *Pendleton Tribune*, March 26, 1898, p. 5.

7. C. A. Angelo, *Sketches of Travel in Oregon and Idaho* (Fairfield, Wash.: Ye Galleon Press, 1988), 48.

8. "Coast to Coast," *Minneapolis Times*, June 2, 1897, p. 5.; "Women Walkers," *Plymouth Republic*, November 19, 1896, p. 6.

9. "Women Globe Trotters," p. 1.

10. Ibid.

11. Ibid.

12. Ibid.

13. "It Continues to Rise," *Idaho Daily Statesman*, June 3, 1896, p. 2.

14. "On a Long Walk," *Idaho Daily Statesman*, June 5, 1896, p. 3.

15. "For Equal Suffrage," *Idaho Daily Statesman*, June 6, 1896, p. 3.

16. "On a Long Walk," p. 3.

9 | Hot, Hungry, and Hopeful

1. "Coast to Coast," *Minneapolis Times*, June 2, 1897, p. 5.

2. "Women Pedestrians," *Daily Sun Leader*, August 27, 1896, p. 4.

3. "From Spokane to New York," *Deseret Evening News*, July 11, 1896, p. 5.

4. "Women Walkers," *Minneapolis Tribune*, June 2, 1897, p. 4.

5. T.T. Williams, *Refuge* (New York: Vintage Books, 1992), p. 70.

6. "From Spokane to New York," p. 5.

7. Ibid.

8. John S. McCormick, "Temple Square," Utah History Encyclopedia, http://historytogo.utah.gov/slcl.html [2002].

9. "From Spokane to New York," p. 5.

10. Ibid.

11. "Women Should Have Leg Freedom," *The Chicago Tribune*, November 1, 1896, p. 1.

12. Ibid.

13. M. Knauff, "The Move Towards Rational Dress," http://www.mpmbooks.com/amelia/RATIONAL.HTM, [October 17, 2001].

14. "Women and Short Skirts," *Sun*, April 30, 1897, p. 3.

15. J.J. Lorence, *Enduring Visions Readings* (Lexington, Mass.: D.C. Heath and Company, 1993), 87.

16. Ibid.

17. Ibid.

10 | Night Terrors

1. "Fair Tramps from the West," *Lebanon Evening News*, December 19, 1896, p. 1.

2. Ibid.

3. "Walked from Pacific Coast," *New York Twice-a-Week World*, December 24, 1896, p. 6.

4. "Fair Tramps from the West," p. 1.

5. C. Moulton, *Roadside History of Wyoming* (Missoula, Mont.: Mountain Press Publishing Co., 1995), 277.

6. Ibid., 243.

7. "Women Pedestrians," *Daily Sun Leader*, August 27, 1896, p. 4.

8. "Women Walkers," *Minneapolis Tribune*, June 2, 1897, p. 4.

9. "Walked from Pacific Coast," p. 6.

10. P. Glad, *McKinley, Bryan and the People* (New York: J.B. Lippincott Company, 1964).

11. L. Ashby, *William Jennings Bryan: Champion of Democracy* (Boston: Twayne Publishers, 1987), 57.

12. Ibid., 62.

13. Ibid., 64.

14. Ibid., 61.

15. "Women Walkers," p. 4.

11 | "New Women's" Actions and Old Victorian Attitudes

1. "Untitled," *Greeley Tribune*, September 3, 1896, p. 1.

2. Ibid.

3. "Women Walkers Reach Plymouth," *Plymouth Republic*, November 19, 1896, p. 6.

4. "Walking to Win," *Des Moines Register*, October 17, 1896, p. 2.

5. "Coast to Coast," *Minneapolis Times*, June 2, 1897, p. 5.

6. Linda Hasselstrom, Gaydell Collier, and Nancy Curtis, *Leaning into the Wind* (New York: Houghton Mifflin Company, 1997), 18.

7. "Fair Tramps from the West," *Lebanon Evening News*, December 19, 1896, p. 1.

8. "Came from Spokane Afoot," *New York Times*, December 24, 1896, p. 9.

9. J. Frost et al., "Why Did Colorado Suffragists Succeed in Winning the Right to Vote in 1893 and Not in 1877?" http://womhist.binghamton.edu/colosuff/intro.htm [June 2002].

10. *Dictionary of American History*, Rev. Ed., s.v. "Cripple Creek Strikes."

11. "Women Walkers Reach Plymouth," p. 6.

12. "Walked from Pacific Coast," *New York Twice-a-Week World*, December 24, 1896, p. 6.

13. Dahn Shaulis, "Pedestriennes: Newsworthy but Controversial Women in Sporting Entertainment," *Journal of Sport History* 26 (1), Spring 1999: 32. See this extensive research on the international phenomenon of nineteenth-century women walkers that demonstrated their strength and endurance through sporting contests and their eventual marginalization after years of competition because Victorian beliefs conflicted with the development of physical culture for women. In Shaulis's journal article, he references Estby's walk across America and refers to one other female pedestrian, Spanish immigrant Zoe Gayton, who achieved a transcontinental walk from California to New York accompanied by two men in 1891. For her achievement, she won a $2000 wager (*New York Times*, March 28, 1891).

14. *Women's Journal*, December 30, 1876, p. 421.

15. "Pedestriennes," 41.

16. *Chicago Tribune*, March 11, 1879, p. 9.

17. "Pedestriennes," 43.

18. S. Stage, *Female Complaints: Lydia Pinkham and the Business of Women's Medicine* (New York: W.W. Norton & Company, 1979).

19. H. Green, *The Light in the Home* (New York: Pantheon Books, 1983), 117.

20. P. Vertinksy, "Feminist Charlotte Perkins Gilman's Pursuit of Health and Physical Fitness as a Strategy for Emancipation," *Journal of Sport History* 16 (1), 1989: 13. This was also known as the "Age of the Womb" by some doctors who were quite concerned over women's nervous ailments. As Dr. George Beard wrote in 1879, "It seems almost impossible for

any woman to suffer from general neurasthenia without developing sooner or later some trouble of the womb or of the ovary." When Helga needed to testify of her "problems to the womb" at her trial after the debilitating fall on Riverside Ave., her actions showed that a "semi-invalid" condition held no status for a busy mother. The short story "The Yellow Wallpaper" by Charlotte Perkins Gilman in 1892 creatively portrays the effects of the medical treatment given to wealthier women who required complete bed rest.

21. From a November 15, 1884, letter from Jane Addams to her stepbrother George, in G. Diliberto, *A Useful Woman* (New York: Scribner, 1999), 110.

22. J.J. Lorence, *Enduring Visions Reading* (Lexington, Mass.: D.C. Heath and Company, 1993), 85.

23. "Women Walkers Reach Plymouth Saturday Night," *Plymouth Republic*, November 19, 1896, p. 6.

24. Ibid.

12 | AN ELECTRIFYING PRESIDENTIAL ELECTION

1. L. Ashby, *William Jennings Bryan: Champion of Democracy* (Boston, Mass.: Twayne Publishers, 1987), 62.

2. P. Glad, *McKinley, Bryan and the People* (New York: J.B. Lippincott Company, 1964), 176.

3. L Ashby, *William Jennings Bryan*, 64.

4. Ibid., 41–71.

5. Ibid., 53.

6. R. Edwards and S. DeFeo, "1896: The Presidential Campaign. Cartoons & Commentary," http://iberia.vassar.edu/1896/1896home.html [June 2002].

7. L. Ashby, *William Jennings Bryan*, 69.

8. "Women Walkers," *Minneapolis Tribune*, June 2, 1897, p. 4.

9. Ibid.

10. "Mrs. William J. Bryan," *New York Sunday World*, August 23, 1896, p. 17.

11. "Women Walkers," p. 4.

12. "More Pedestrians," *Des Moines Leader*, October 15, 1896, p. 5.

13. "Walking to Win $10,000," *Des Moines Register*, October 17, 1896, p. 2.

14. Ibid.

15. "They are Here," *Daily Iowa Capital*, October 17, 1896, p. 5.

16. Ibid.

17. Ibid.

18. "Two Women Afoot," *Davenport Democrat*, October 24, 1896, p. 1.

13 | EARNING THEIR OWN WAY

1. "Two Women Tramps," *Lebanon Daily News*, December 19, 1896, p. 1.

2. P. Glad, *McKinley, Bryan, and the People: Critical Periods of History* (New York: J.B. Lippincott Company, 1964).

3. Ibid., 179.

4. Ibid., 170.

5. L. Ashby, *William Jennings Bryan: Champion of Democracy* (Boston: Twayne Publishers, 1987), 67.

6. Ibid., 67.

7. Ibid., 41.

8. "Are Tramping to New York," *Chicago Evening Post*, November 7, 1896, p. 1.

9. Ibid.

10. C. Schwantes, *Coxey's Army: An American Odyssey* (Moscow, Idaho: University of Idaho Press, 1994), 13.

11. "Diphtheria in Chicago," *New York Twice-a-Week World*, November 23, 1896, p. 1.

12. G. Diliberto, *A Useful Woman: The Early Life of Jane Addams* (New York: Scribner, 1999), 17. Also, see Ronald White and C. Howard Hopkin's *Social Gospel: Religion and Reform in Changing America* (Temple University Press, 1975).

13. "Walk for $10,000," *Chicago Journal*, November 7, 1896, p. 1.

14. Ibid.

15. "Women Walkers Reach Plymouth Saturday Night,"
    Plymouth Republic, November 19, 1896, p. 6.

16. Ibid.

17. Ibid.

18. "Walking for Pay," *Fort Wayne Sentinel*, November 18, 1896, p. 1.

19. Ibid.

20. "On a Long Walk," *Idaho Daily Statesman*, June 5, 1896, p. 3.

14│A RUSH TO THE FINISH

1. "Mother and Daughter," *Ohio State Journal*, November 24,
   1896, p. 3.

2. H.W. Brands, *The Reckless Decade: America in the 1890s*
   (New York: St. Martin's Press, 1995), 160–176.

3. C. Schwantes, *Coxey's Army: An American Odyssey*
   (Moscow, Idaho: University of Idaho Press, 1994), 45.

4. Ibid., 55.

5. Ibid., 237–38.

6. H.W. Brands, *The Reckless Decade*, 173.

7. C. Schwantes, *Coxey's Army*, 177–185.

8. Ibid., 260.

9. "Women Walkers," *Minneapolis Tribune*, June 2, 1897, p. 4.

10. "Coast to Coast," *Minneapolis Times*, June 2, 1897, p. 5.

11. "The White House: First Ladies' Gallery," http://www.white-
    house.gov/history/firstladies [2002].

12. "Coast to Coast," *Minneapolis Times*; Darillyn Bahr, "Coast
    to Coast," School Research Report, Wilbur, Wash., 1977.

13. "Spokane Callers at McKinleys," *Spokesman-Review*,
    December 1, 1896.

14. Ibid.

15. "A Long, Long Walk," *Alliance Daily Review*, November 30, 1896, p. 4.

16. Ibid.

15 | The Impossible Happens

1. "Walking for $10,000," *Harrisburg Telegraph*, December 5, 1896, p. 1.

2. "Fair Tramps from the West," *Lebanon Evening News*, December 19, 1896, p. 1.

3. "Walked from Pacific Coast," *New York Twice-a-Week World*, December 24, 1896, p. 6.

4. Ibid.

5. "Two Women Tramps," *Lebanon Daily News*, December 19, 1896, p. 2.

6. "Afoot from Spokane," *Reading Times*, December 19, 1896, p. 2.

7. Ibid.

8. "Walked from Pacific Coast," p. 6.

9. Ibid.

10. Ibid.

11. "Came from Spokane Afoot," *New York Times*, December 24, 1896, p. 9.

12. "Two Women's Long Tramp," *New York Herald*, December 23, 1896, p. 10.

13. "The Estby's Reach New York," *Spokesman-Review*, December 24, 1896, p. 2.

14. "Mrs. Estby and Her Daughter Walked Armed from Spokane," *World*, December 25, 1896, p. 2.

15. Ibid.

16. Ibid.

17. Ibid.

1. Nancy Woloch, *Women and the American Experience* (New York: Alfred A. Knopf, 1984), 236.

2. Ibid., 234.

3. "Coast to Coast," *Minneapolis Times*, June 2, 1897, p. 4.

4. Ibid.

5. "Auction," *Standard Union*, January 12, 1897, p. 1.

6. "Walked Here from Spokane: Mrs. Estby Tells a Harrowing Tale of Eight Years of Tribulation," *Sun*, May 2, 1897, p. 1.

7. Arlene Coulson, "Research Notes on Helga Estby's Family," Whitworth College History Project, 1986.

8. "Walked Here from Spokane," p. 1.

9. Ida Estby, Oral History at Cheney Cowles Museum, Spokane, Wash., 1973.

10. "Letters," Family Artifacts, 1893.

11. R.N. Tooker, *The Disease of Children and their Homeopathic Treatment: Textbook for Students, Colleges, and Practitioners*, 2nd ed. (Chicago: Gross & Delbridge Company, 1898).

12. Thelma Portch, first interview by author, Almira, Wash., 1983.

13. Ibid.

14. "Women Travelers Ask for Aid," *New York Daily Tribune*, May 2, 1897, p. 8.

15. Ibid.

16. Ibid.

17. Ibid.

18. "Walked Here from Spokane," p. 1.

19. T. Portch, first interview.

1. "Coast to Coast," *Minneapolis Times*, June 2, 1897, p. 4.

2. Ibid.

3. "Women Walkers," *Minneapolis Tribune*, June 2, 1897, p. 4.

4. "Coast to Coast," p. 4.

5. "Women Walkers," p. 4

6. Ibid.

7. "Women Walkers," p. 4.

8. "Coast to Coast," p. 4.

10. Ibid.

11. "Women Walkers," p. 4.

12. "Coast to Coast," p. 4.

13. "On a Long Walk," *Idaho Daily Statesman*, June 3, 1896, p. 3.

14. R.C. Sahr, Consumer Price Index Conversion Factors: 1800–2012. Political Science Department, Oregon State University, April 2, 2002.

15. "Two Women's Long Walk," *San Francisco Examiner*, May 5, 1896, p. 3.

16. "Are Walking for Wages," *Walla Walla Union*, May 17, 1896, p. 4.

17. "Fair Tramps from West," *Lebanon Daily News*, December 19, 1896, p. 1.

18. Lyndia Carter, "Ogden Defeats Salt Lake City in a War of the Wheels," *History Blazer*, http://historytogo.utah.gov/ogdenwheels.html [December, 1996].

19. The mention of any Spokane connection has been discovered in only two newspapers in Indiana, and only one mentions a "wealthy Spokane suffragette"; all other newspaper accounts refer to a New York or eastern sponsor or "parties." Women in the Washington Territory received the right to vote in 1883, but lost this when Washington became a state in 1888. Interest in women's suffrage came in waves after this, with very limited interest before 1898 and a great surge beginning

in 1907, which Helga supported. However, prior to 1896, some women committed to the temperance movement also met occasionally on the suffrage issue. One potential contact in Spokane was Dr. Mary Latham who testified in the lawsuit against the city during Helga's illness. As early as 1890, Dr. Latham wrote a letter to the editor of the *Spokesman-Review* that referred to a request to promote suffrage in Spokane from a national leader of suffrage, Matilda Joslyn Gage. A prominent physician, married to another physician, she could have qualified as "wealthy" in Helga's eyes. She had professional contacts in the East and could have connected Helga to the New York sponsor, however, no records indicate she continued as an active suffragette. Often women committed to women's suffrage before 1898 waged their battles in the fashion of a "Still Hunt," a private campaign that was not easily visible to outsiders. This tactic, advocated openly by prominent Pacific Northwest suffragist Abigail Scott Duniway, provided a discreet method of promoting women's rights to the ballot. But it also leads to an incomplete record of local suffragettes. Nancy Engle's excellent doctoral research on Spokane suffragettes speaks to this issue ("Debating Suffrage? The 'Still Hunt' in Spokane, 1898" in an April 27, 2001, paper). The most famous wealthy suffragette from Spokane, May Arkwright Hutton, gained enormous riches from her silver mining claims, but in 1896 she still lived in Wallace, Idaho, and had not yet struck it rich. The reference to Spokane may have been a reporting error, although it is conceivable that a woman in Spokane connected her to an Eastern party.

18 | LOST AND FOUND

1. Arlene Coulson, "Research Notes on Helga Estby's Family," Whitworth College History Project, 1986, Death Certificates.

2. Nels Siverson interview, 1986. See also the work of A. Anastasio, "Port Haven: A Changing Northwestern Community," *Institute of Agricultural Sciences*, Bulletin 616, Washington State University (1960), 1–44. As late as the 1950s, in research on a Scandinavian community of Poulsbo, Washington, the key importance of family life was cited and there was disapproval of any wife not fulfilling perceived responsi-

bilities. The Norwegian-American literature of the period presented a consistent theme of the patriarchal nature of the husband's authority in the home (see J.N. Buckely, "Martha Ostenso: A Norwegian-American Immigrant Novelist," *Norwegian-American Studies and Records* 28 (1979): 69–81). As one writer noted, "The Scandinavian husband's authority in both Old- and New-World settings . . . was dominated by the father, whose authority over both wife and children in the home country was nearly absolute" (79). Ole's inability to stop his wife's action could be construed by his neighboring community as "abdicating his headship."

3. "Walk to New York," *Spokesman-Review*, May 5, 1896, p. 5.

4. J.J. Lorence, *Enduring Visions Readings* (Lexington, Mass.: D.C. Heath and Company, 1993), 83.

5. Darillyn Bahr, "Coast to Coast," School Research Report, Wilbur, Wash., 1977, 14.

6. Thelma Portch, first and second interview by author, Almira, Wash., 1984, 1986.

7. D.C. Jack, *Silencing the Self* (Cambridge, Mass.: Harvard University Press, 1991).

8. A. Coulson, "Research Notes," 1986, Mortgage Book.

9. T. Portch, second interview.

10. D. Bahr, "Coast to Coast," 16.

11. H. Portch, interview with grandson-in-law by author, Spokane, Wash., 1994.

12. T. Portch, first interview.

13. Ibid.

14. Ibid.

15. Norma Lee, interview with granddaughter by author, Spokane, Wash., 1992.

16. T. Portch, second interview; Wanda Estby Michalek, phone interview with granddaughter-in-law by author, June 25, 1996.

17. D. Bahr, "Coast to Coast."

18. Doug Bahr, "Grandma Walks from Coast to Coast," Eighth grade Essay, Wilbur, Wash., 1984.

1. E. Stone, *Black Sheep and Kissing Cousins: How our Family Stories Shape Us* (New York: Times Books/Random House, 1988), 8.

2. Electronic-mail message to author from a confidential source reflecting on the impact of the silencing of family stories, Spokane, Wash., November 15, 2000.

3. See the pivotal work of Appleby, Hunt, and Jacob, *Telling the Truth About History* (New York: Norton, 1994) and E. Foner, ed., *The New American History* (Philadelphia: Temple University Press, 1990). The Women's West Conference in 1983 began a new era of historical inquiry and scholarship that led to the publication of Armitage and Jameson's *The Women's West* (University of Oklahoma, 1987) and a flood of research and publication on women's lives. This emergence of a new western history now includes previously marginalized women from multicultural backgrounds and offers a far richer picture of women in the American West, as exemplified in the research presented at the Women's Western History Conference in 2000.

4. J. Rosenblatt, "Charred Manuscripts Tell Zora Neale Hurston's Poignant and Powerful Story," *The Chronicle of Higher Education*, B4–5.

5. H.W. Brands, *The Reckless Decade: America in the 1890s* (New York: St. Martin's Press, 2002), x.

6. *Webster's New World Dictionary*, 3rd College ed., s.v. "shame."

7. L. Seppa-Salisbury, psychologist, interview by author, 1996.

8. D.C. Jack, *Silencing the Self: Women and Depression* (Cambridge, Mass.: Harvard University Press, 1991), 11.

9. Ibid.

10. M. Houston and C. Kramarae, "Speaking from Silence: Methods of Silencing and of Resistance," *Discourse & Society* 214 (1991): 388.

11. L. Rosenfeld, "Self-disclosure Avoidance: Why I Am Afraid to Tell You Who I Am," *Communications Monographs* 46 (1) (1979): 63–74.

12. D. Goleman, *Vital Lies, Simple Truths* (New York: Simon & Schuster, 1985), 218, 244.

13. J. Bradshaw, *Family Secrets* (New York: Bantam, 1995).

14. L. S. Smart, "Parental Bereavement in Anglo American History," *Omega* 28 (1): 49–61.

15. M. Vicinus, *Suffer and Be Still: Women in the Victorian Age* (Bloomington: Indiana University Press, 1973).

16. L.S. Smart, "Parental Bereavement in Anglo American History," 57.

17. Thelma Portch, first and second interviews by author, 1984, 1986; Wanda Estby Michalek, interview by author, June 25, 1996.

18. M. Vicinus, *Suffer and Be Still*.

19. Tillie Olsen, *Silences* (New York: Dell Publishing Co., 1965), 35.

Bibliography

Addams, J. *Twenty Years at Hull House*. New York: Macmillan, 1910.

"Afoot from Spokane, Washington," *Reading Times*, 19 December 1896, p. 2.

Akerman, S. "The Psychology of Migration." *American Studies in Scandinavia* 1 (1978): 47–56.

"A Long Journey," *Fort Wayne Gazette*, 19 November 1896, p. 3.

Alpern, S., J. Antler, E. Perry, and I. Scobie, eds. *The Challenge of Feminist Biography: Writing the Lives of Modern American Women*. Urbana: University of Illinois Press, 1992.

Anastasio, A. "Port Haven: A Changing Northwestern Community." *Institute of Agricultural Sciences* Bulletin 616: Washington State University, 1–44.

Appleby, J., L. Hunt, and M. Jacob. *Telling the Truth about History*. New York: Norton, 1994.

"Applied for Assistance," *Brooklyn Daily Eagle*, 2 May 1897.

"Are Near Their Journey's End," *Spokesman-Review*, 23 December 1896, p. 1.

"Are Walking for Wages," *Walla Walla Union*, 17 May 1896, p. 4.

Armitage, S. "Revisiting 'The Gentle Tamers Revisited': The Problems and Possibilities of Western Women's History—An Introduction." *Pacific Historical Review* 61, no. 4 (1992): 459–462.

——. "Here's to the Women: Western Women Speak Up." *The Journal of American History* (September 1996): 551–559.

Armitage S., and E. Jameson, eds. *The Women's West*. Norman: University of Oklahoma Press, 1987.

Armitage S., E. Jameson, and J. Jansen. "The New Western History: Another Perspective." *Journal of the West* 32 (July 1993): 5.

Ashby, L. *William Jennings Bryan: Champion of Democracy*. Boston: Twayne Publishers, 1987.

"Auction," *Brooklyn Standard Union*, 12 January 1897, p. 1.

Bahr, Dorothy, and Daryll Bahr. *Artifacts of Estby Family: Portraits, Scrapbooks, Letters, Artifacts*. Wilbur and Spokane, Wash., 1880–1930.

Bahr, Darillyn. "Coast to Coast." School report. Wilbur, Wash., 1977.

Bahr, Doug. "Grandma Walks from Coast to Coast." History Day Contest report. Wilbur, Wash., 1984.

Bancroft, H.H. *Bancroft's Works: Nevada, Colorado and Wyoming, XXV*. San Francisco: The History Company Publishers, 1890.

———. *Bancroft's Works: History of Utah, XXVI*. San Francisco, The History Company Publishers, 1890.

Barzun, J., and H. Graff. *The Modern Researcher*. 5th ed. Fort Worth: Harcourt, Brace Jovanovich, 1977.

Becher, E.T. *Spokane Corona: Eras and Empires*. Spokane: Self-published, 1974.

Belenky, M., L. Bond, and J. Weinstock. *A Tradition That Has No Name*. New York: Basic Books, Inc., 1997.

Belenky, M., B. Clinchy, N. Goldberger, and J. Tarule. *Women's Ways of Knowing*. New York: Basic Books, Inc., 1986.

Birkett, D. *Spinsters Abroad: Victorian Lady Explorers*. New York: Blackwell, 1989.

Bjork, K. *West of the Great Divide: Norwegian Migration to the Pacific Coast: 1847–1893*. Northfield: Norwegian-American Historical Association, 1958.

Blackburn, G., and S. Ricards. "A Demographic History of the West: Manistee County, Michigan, 1860," *The Journal of American History* 57, no. 3 (1970): 600–618.

"Black Friday," *Canby (Minn.) News*, 19 July 1885, p. 3A.

Blegen, T.C. *Norwegian Migration to America (2)*. North-field, Minn.: The Norwegian-American Historical Association, 1940.

Blegen, T.C., ed. *Land of Their Choice: The Immigrants Write Home*. Minneapolis: University of Minnesota Press, 1955.

Bowen, C.D. *Adventures of a Biographer*. Boston: Little, Brown, 1959.

Bradshaw, J. *Family Secrets*. New York: Bantam, 1995.

Brands, H.W. *The Reckless Decade: America in the 1890s*. New York: St. Martin's Press, 1995.

Brinkman, M.S., and W.T. Morgan. *Light from the Hearth: Central Minnesota Pioneers and Early Architecture*. St. Cloud, Minn.: North Star Press, 1982.

Buckely, J.N. "Martha Ostenso: A Norwegian-American Immigrant Novelist." *Norwegian-American Studies and Records* 28 (1979): 69–81.

"Call grand jury," *Spokesman-Review*, 11 December 1903, p. 1.

"Came from Spokane Afoot," *New York Times*, 24 December 1896, p. 9.

Carrere, J.F. *Spokane Falls Washington Territory and its Tributary Country*. Spokane, Wash.: City Council and Board of Trade, 1889.

Cather, W. *My Ántonia*. Boston: Houghton Mifflin Company, 1918.

"Census," *City of Spokane*, 1896.

Circular No. 1. Minnesota State Board of Health, 1880.

"Coast to Coast," *Minneapolis Times*, 2 June 1897, p. 5.

Cott, N.F. *The Bonds of Womanhood: "Women's Sphere" in New England, 1780–1835*. New Haven, Conn.: Yale University Press, 1977.

Coulson, A. Unpublished research notes on Helga Estby family. Whitworth College, 1986.

Cummins, M.S. *The Lamplighter*. Vol. 6. 1854. Reprint, New Brunswick: Rutgers University Press, 1988.

Dahlie, J. *A Social History of Scandinavian Immigration, Washington State, 1895–1910*. Pullman: Washington State University Press, 1967.

Davis, L.G. *A Diphtheria Epidemic in the Early Eighties*. Sleepy Eye: Minnesota Medical Report, 1934.

Diliberto, G. *A Useful Woman: The Early Life of Jane Addams*. New York: Scribner, 1999.

Estby, I. *Oral History at Cheney Cowles Museum*. Spokane, Wash., 1973. Daughter of Helga and Ole Estby.

"The Estby's Reach New York," *Spokesman-Review*, 24 December 1896, p. 2.

Fahey, J. "The Million Dollar Corner: The Development of Downtown Spokane, 1890–1920." *Pacific Northwest Quarterly* 62 (April 1971): 77–85.

——. *The Inland Empire: Unfolding Years, 1879–1929*. Seattle: University of Washington Press, 1986.

"Fair Tramps' Long Trip," *New York Twice-a-Week World*, 27 November 1896, p. 1.

Fargo, L.F. *Spokane Story*. New York: Columbia University Press, 1950.

"For a Long Tramp," *Spokane Daily Chronicle*, 5 May 1896, p. 1.

Frederick, B., and S. McLeod, eds. *Women and the Journey: Female Travel Experience*. Pullman: Washington State University Press, 1993.

"From Spokane to New York," *Salt Lake City Deseret Evening News*, 11 July 1896, p. 5.

Frost, J., et al. "Why Did Colorado Suffragists Succeed in Winning the Right to Vote in 1893 and Not in 1877?" http://womhisto.binghamton.edu/colosuff/intro.htm [2002].

Gale's Quotations: Who Said What. Ver. 1.0. CD-ROM. W.E.B. DuBois, 1903.

Geddes, P. *The Evolution of Sex*. London: W. Scott, 1889.

Glad, P.W. *McKinley, Bryan, and the People*. New York: J.B. Lippincott Company, 1964.

Goleman, D. *Vital Lies, Simple Truths*. New York: Simon & Schuster, 1985.

The Greeley (Colorado) Tribune, 3 September 1896, p. 1.

Green, H., et al. *The Light of the Home: An Intimate View of the Lives of Women in Victorian America*. New York: Pantheon Books, 1983.

Griffin, S. *A Chorus of Stones*. New York: Doubleday, 1992.

Gulliksen, O. "Travel Narratives, Popular Religious Literature, Autobiography: N.N. Ronning's Contribution to Norwegian-American Culture." *Norwegian-American Studies* 33 (1992): 165–188.

Hamalian, L., ed. *Ladies on the Loose: Women Travellers of the 18th and 19th Centuries*. New York: Dodd, Mead, 1981.

Hanne, M. *Power of the Story*. Providence: Berghahn Books, 1994.

Heilbrun, C.G. *Writing a Woman's Life*. New York: W.W. Norton & Company, 1988.

Herriges, R.P. *Fire on the Prairie: Memories of Lac Zui Parle*. Madison, Minn.: The Heritage Press, 1980.

"History of Manistee County," *Minnesota Historical Society Files* (1996): p. 8–9.

Holmquist, J.D., ed. *They Chose Minnesota: A Survey of the State's Ethnic Groups*. St. Paul: Minnesota Historical Press, 1981.

Holt, L.E. *Diseases of Infancy and Childhood: For the Use of Students and Practitioners of Medicine*. New York: D. Appleton and Company, 1897.

Hook, H., and F. McGuire. *Spokane Falls Illustrated: The Metropolis of Eastern Washington*. Minneapolis: Frank L. Thresher, 1889.

Houston, M., and C. Kramarae. "Speaking from Silence: Methods of Silencing and of Resistance." *Discourse and Society* 214 (1991): 387–399.

Hoxtel, A. Interview by author. 1995. Lived in Estby house as a child.

Hustvedt, L. Interview by author. St. Olaf College, Minn., 6 June 1996. Secretary of Norwegian-American Historical Association.

"In Short Skirts," *Fort Wayne News*, 18 November 1896, p. 1.

Jack, D.C. *Silencing the Self: Women and Depression*. Cambridge: Harvard University Press, 1991.

Jeffrey, J.R. *Frontier Women: The Trans-Mississippi West: 1840–1880*. New York: Hill and Wang, 1979.

Jenkins, P., and B. Jenkins. *The Walk West: A Walk across America 2*. Carmel, N.Y.: Guideposts, 1981.

Jensen, J., and D. Miller. "The Gentle Tamers Revisited: New Approaches to the History of Women in the American West." *Pacific Historical Review* 49 (1980): 173–213.

"Journey Almost Ended," *New York World*, 23 December 1896.

"The Jury in the Estley [*sic*] Suit," *Spokane Falls Review*, 21 February 1889, p. 4.

Kaplan, L.J. *No Voice is Ever Wholly Lost*. New York: Simon & Schuster, 1995.

King, M.P. *Memories of a Prairie Girlhood*. Minnesota: Canby City Library Memoir, 1960.

Lagerquist, L.D. *In America the Men Milk the Cows: Factors of Gender, Ethnicity, and Religion in the Americanization of Norwegian-American Women*. Brooklyn: Carlson Publishing, 1991.

Lea, H.C. *A Treatise of the Diseases of Infancy and Childhood*. 2nd ed. Philadelphia: Henry C. Lea, 1872.

Lee, Norma. Interview by author. Spokane, Wash., 1992. Granddaugher of Helga Estby.

Letters. Thelma Portch Collection, 1893.

Limerick, P.N., C.A. Milner II, C.E. Rankin, eds. *Trails: Toward a New Western History*. Lawrence: University of Kansas Press, 1991.

"Lives Wrecked by Wheeling," *San Francisco Examiner*, 1 July 1896, p. 1.

"Local News," *Shoshone Journal*, 26 June 1896.

"Long Tramp for Two Women," *New York World*, 6 May 1896, p. 1.

Lorence, J.J. *Enduring Visions Readings*. Lexington, Mass.: D.C. Heath and Company, 1993.

Lovoll, O.S. *The Promise of America: A History of the Norwegian-American People*. Minneapolis: University of Minnesota Press, 1983.

Luchetti, C. *Women of the West*. St. George: Antelope Island Press, 1982.

Malcolm, J. *The Silent Woman*. New York: Random House, 1993.

McBride, E. Interview with author. 1995. Family lived in Estby home.

McCormick, J.S. "Temple Square." http://historytogo.utah.gov/ slc1.html [October 2002].

McNair, S. *Nebraska*. New York: Grolier Publishing Co., 1999.

Meier, P. *Bring Warm Clothes: Letters and Photos from Minnesota's Past*. Minneapolis: *Minneapolis Tribune*, 1981.

Michalek, W. Interview by author. Phone. 25 June 1996. Granddaughter-in-law of Helga Estby.

Middleton, D. *Victorian Lady Travellers*. London: Routledge and Kegan Paul, 1965.

"Minnesota Storm Damage," *Canby (Minn.) News*, 24 June 1885, p. 1.

Miscovitch, D. Interview by author. 1994. With Miscovitch's mother who lived in Estby home at Mica.

Montgomery Ward & Co. Spring and Summer 1895. Catalogue No. 57. Toronto: Dover Press.

"More Pedestrians," *Des Moines Leader*, 15 October 1896, p. 5.

"Mother and Daughter," *Ohio State Journal*, 24 November 1896, p. 3.

Moulton, C. *Roadside History of Wyoming*. Missoula, Mont.: Mountain Press Publishing Company, 1995.

"Mrs. Estby and Her Daughter Walk Armed from Spokane," *New York World*, 25 December 1896, p. 2.

"Mrs. Estby's Tramp Ended," *Chronicle*, 24 December 1896, p. 1.

"Mrs. H. Estby and Daughter," *Warsaw Daily Times*, 18 November 1896, p. 2.

Mutel, F.M., and J.C. Emerick. *From Grassland to Glacier: The Natural History of Colorado and the Surrounding Region*. Boulder: Johnson Books, 1984.

Narvestad, J. *The History of Yellow Medicine County*. Granite Falls: Yellow Medicine County Historical Society, 1972.

National Archives of Norway (*Riksarkivet*). *Birth, Christening, Ship Records*. Oslo, Norway, 1860s.

Olsen, T. *Silences*. New York: Dell Publishing Co., 1965.

"On a Long Walk," *Idaho Daily Statesman*, 5 June 1896, p. 3.

"On Their Journey," *Weekly Bedrock Democrat*, 1 June 1896.

Oslo City Records. "Norwegian Family Records." Oslo, Norway. 1860s.

Papero, D. *Bowen Family Systems Theory*. Needham Heights, Mass.: Allyn and Bacon, 1990.

Pascoe, P. "Western Women at the Crossroads." In Limerick, Milner, and Rankin, eds. *Trails: Toward a New Western History*, 1991.

Peavy, L., and U. Smith. *Women in Waiting in the Westward Movement*. Norman: University of Oklahoma Press, 1994.

Portch, H. Interview by author. Spokane, Wash., 1994. Grandson-in-law of Helga Estby.

Portch, T. Interview by author. Almira, Wash., 1984. Granddaughter of Helga Estby.

———. Interview by author. Almira, Wash., 1986. Second interview.

Pratt, O.C. *The Story of Spokane*. Self-published: Spokane City Library, 1948.

Qualey, C.C. "A Typical Norwegian Settlement: Spring Grove, Minnesota." *Norwegian American Studies and Records* 9 (1936).

Raaen, A. *Grass of the Earth: The Story of a Norwegian Immigrant Family in Dakota*. St. Paul: Minnesota Historical Society Press, 1950.

Rasmussen, J.E. *New Land, New Lives: Scandinavian Immigrants to the Pacific Northwest*. Northfield, Minn.: Norwegian-American Historical Association, 1963.

———. "'The Best Place on Earth for Women': The American Experience of Aasta Hansteen." *Norwegian American Studies* 32 (1986): 245–266.

Rettman, J. "Prostitution in Spokane, Washington: 1889–1908." Master's thesis, Eastern Washington University, 1994.

Rich, A.C. *On Lies, Secrets, and Silence*. New York: Norton, 1979.

Ricouer, P. *Time and Narrative*. Vol. 1 & 2. Chicago: University of Chicago Press, 1984.

Robinson, P. *Sinners and Saints: A Tour across the States and Round Them with Three Months among the Mormons*. Boston: Roberts Brothers, 1883.

"Rockford," *Spokesman-Review*, 14 February 1889, p. 1.

"Rockford," *Rockford Realm*. 1 January 1890, p. 1.

Rolvaag, O.E. *Giants on the Earth*. New York: Harper and Row, 1955.

Rose, A.P. *An Illustrated History of Yellow Medicine County, Minnesota*. Marshall, Minn.: Northern History Publishing Company, 1914.

Rosenblatt, J. "Charred Manuscripts Tell Zora Neale Hurston's Poignant and Powerful Story." *The Chronicle of Higher Education* (5 June 1991): B4–5.

Rosenfeld, L. "Self-disclosure Avoidance: Why I Am Afraid to Tell You Who I Am." *Communications Monographs* 46, no. 1 (1979): 63–74.

Rothman, S.M. *Woman's Proper Place: A History of Changing Ideals and Practices, 1870 to the Present*. New York: Basic Books, 1978.

Rudd, C.D. "Beret and the Prairie in Giants in the Earth." *Norwegian American Studies* 28 (1975): 217–245.

Russell, M. *The Blessings of a Good Thick Skirt: Women Travellers and Their World*. London: Collins, 1986.

Sandro, G.O. *The Immigrants' Trek*. Self-published: Minnesota, 1929.

Scharff, V. "Else Surely We Shall All Hang Separately: The Politics of Western Women's History." *Pacific Historical Review* 61 (1992): 535–555.

Schwantes, C.A. *Coxey's Army*. Moscow: University of Idaho Press, 1994.

Seller, M.S., ed. *Immigrant Women*. Philadelphia: Temple University Press, 1981.

Seppa-Salisbury, L. Interview by author. 1996. A psychologist's perspective on shame.

Settler's Guide to Homes in the Northwest: Being a Handbook of Spokane Falls, W.T. Spokane, Wash.: Spokane Falls Evening Review Book and Job Print, 1885.

Shaulis, Dahn. "Pedestriennes: Newsworthy but Controversial Women in Sporting Entertainment," *Journal of Sport History* 26 (1), 1999.

Shoshone Journal, 26 June 1896.

Siverson, N. Interviews by author. 1986, 1993. Neighbor of Estbys.

Slattery, T.J. "An Illustrated History of the Rock Island Arsenal and Arsenal Island." Davenport: Historical Office, 1988.

Slind, M.G., and F.D. Bohm. *Norse to the Palouse: Sagas of the Selbu Norwegians*. Pullman, Wash.: Norlys Press, 1990.

Smart, L.S. "Parental Bereavement in Anglo American History." *Omega* 28, no. 1 (1993): 49–61.

Smith, B.H. "Narrative Versions, Narrative Theories." *Critical Inquiry* 7, no. 1 (1980): 213–236.

"Spokane Caller at McKinley's," *Spokesman-Review*, 1 December 1896, p. 4.

Spokane County Court Records. "Mortgages, Law suits, Deeds, etc.: 1890s–1920."

Spokane Falls Evening Chronicle, 21 September 1886.

"Spokane Falls, Washington Territory: The Metropolis of Eastern Washington and Northern Idaho 1889." Spokane, Wash.: Union Pacific Railroad, 1889.

Stage, S. *Female Complaints: Lydia Pinkham and the Business of Women's Medicine*. New York: W.W. Norton & Company, 1979.

Stearns, P.N. "Girls, Boys, and Emotions: Redefinitions and Historical Change." *The Journal of American History* (June 1993): 37–47.

Stone, E. *Black Sheep and Kissing Cousins: How Our Family Stories Shape Us*. New York: Times Books/ Random House, 1988.

"The Story They Told," *San Francisco Chronicle*, 24 December 1896, p. 3.

Stratton, D., ed. *Spokane and the Inland Empire: An Interior Pacific Northwest Anthology*. Pullman: Washington State University Press, 1991.

"Surrounding country," *Realm*, 1 January 1890, p. 1, Supplement.

Theriot, N. *Mothers and Daughters in Nineteenth-Century America*. Lexington: University of Kentucky Press, 1996.

"They Are Here," *Daily Iowa Capital*, 17 October 1896, p. 5.

Tooker, R.N. *The Diseases of Children and their Homeopathic Treatment: Text-book for Students, Colleges and Practitioners*. 2nd ed. Chicago: Gross & Delbridge Company, 1898.

"Tramp to New York," *Spokane Daily Chronicle*, 4 May 1896, p. 2.

Trodd, A. *Domestic Crime in the Victorian Novel*. New York: St. Martin's Press, 1989.

"Two Women Afoot," *Davenport Democrat*, 24 October 1896, p. 1.

"Two Women's Great Tramp," *New York World*, 26 April 1896, p. 24. Photograph.

"Two Women's Long Tramp," *New York Herald*, 23 December 1896, p. 10.

"Two Women's Long Walk," *Examiner*, 5 May 1896.

"Two Women Tramps," *Lebanon (Penn.) Daily News*, 19 December 1896, p. 1.

"Two Women Walkers," *Denver Times*, 11 September 1896, p. 10.

Vertinsky, P. "Feminist Charlotte Perkins Gilman's Pursuit of Health and Physical Fitness as a Strategy for Emancipation." *Journal of Sport History* 16, no. 1 (1989): 5–26.

Veyne, P. *Writing History: Essay on Epistemology*. Middletown: Wesleyan University Press, 1971.

Vicinus, M. *Suffer and Be Still: Women in the Victorian Age*. Bloomington: Indiana University Press, 1973.

"Walk to New York," *Spokesman-Review*, 5 May 1896, p. 5.

"Walked from Pacific Coast," *Minneapolis Tribune*, 2 June 1897, p. 4.

"Walked from Pacific Coast," *New York Twice-a-Week World*, 24 December 1896, p. 6.

"Walked Here from Spokane," *New York Sun*, 2 May 1897.

"Walking for Pay," *Fort Wayne Sentinel*, 18 November 1896, p. 1.

"Walking for $10,000," *Harrisburg Telegraph*, 5 December 1896, p. 1.

"Walking to Win $10,000," *Des Moines Register*, 17 October 1896, p. 2.

Walsh, M. "State of the Art: Women's Place on the American Frontier." *Journal of American Studies* 29, no. 2 (1995): 241–255.

Ware, S. *Still Missing: Amelia Earhart and the Search for Modern Feminism*. New York: W.W. Norton, 1993.

Welter, B. *Dimity Convictions: The American Woman in the 19th Century*. Athens: Ohio University Press, 1976.

"What To Do in a Tornado," *Canby (Minn.) News*, 15 May 1885, p. 4.

Woloch, N. *Women and the American Experience*. New York: Alfred A. Knopf, 1984.

"Woman and Short Skirts," *New York Sun*, 30 April 1897.

"Woman Pedestrian a Loser," *Spokesman-Review*, 19 April 1916, p. 6.

"Woman Should Have Leg Freedom," *Chicago Tribune*, 1
November 1896, p. 1.

"Women's Congress Attracts Crowds," *San Francisco
Chronicle*, 5 May 1896, p. 1.

Women's club authors. *Down Memory Lane*. Mica, Wash.:
Mica Community Publication, 1979.

"Women Globe Trotters," *Weekly Baker City (Ore.)
Bedrock Democrat*, 25 May 1896, p. 1.

"Women of the Week," *New York World*, 26 April 1896, p. 24.

"Women Pedestrians," *Daily Sun Leader*, 27 August 1896, p. 4.

"Women Travellers Ask for Aid," *New York Daily Tribune*,
2 May 1897, p. 8.

"Women Walkers," *Minneapolis Tribune*, 2 June 1897, p. 4.

"Women Walkers Arrive," *New York Herald*, 24 December
1896, p. 7.

"Women Walkers: Reach Plymouth Saturday Night,"
Plymouth Reporter, 19 November 1896, p. 6.

"Women Walkers Stranded," *New York World*, 2 May 1897.

Yellow Medicine County Court Records. *Births, Deaths,
Homestead papers*. 1877–1887.

Index

Acknowledgments

The challenge of reconstructing the lost story of Helga Estby's walk across America more than one hundred years ago required investigative help from all who might hold a remnant of her life. As with so many persons considered "ordinary" in earlier American history, little value was placed on saving any of her historical records.

Thus, I am grateful for each family member, historical society, museum, and community or university library that work diligently as story keepers of ordinary lives. Whenever staff within these regional resources heard of Helga's remarkable unknown achievement, they brought abundant skills, persistence, and a spirit of service to discover what still lay buried. For years of tenacious sleuthing, I especially thank Whitworth College librarians Nancy Bunker and Gail Fielding. Nancy Compau at the Northwest History Room at the Spokane Public Library, Judy Austin at the Idaho Historical Society, and Laura Arksey, Karen DeSeve, and Rayette Wilder from the Cheney Cowles Museum/Northwest Museum of Art and Culture provided excellent assistance at different stages of this research. Staff within historical societies and public libraries in Oregon, Idaho, Utah, Wyoming, Colorado, Illinois, Iowa, Nebraska, Indiana, Ohio, Pennsylvania, and New York contributed valuable knowledge of their local resources. The extensive collection of microfilm newspapers at the Butler Library at Columbia University and the historic personal memoirs donated to the public library in Canby, Minnesota, offered insightful additions to Helga's experiences.

It proved fortuitous that Norwegians place such a high value on careful record keeping and interest in Norwegian-American stories. The staff at the Riksarkivet (National Archives of Norway) gave generous help in researching and translating original documents. The Oslo City Records department, Anne Lise Stafne of Oslo's *Aftenposten* newspaper, and writer and researcher Torbjorn Greipsland added other vital Norwegian resources. In America, Lloyd Hustvedt and Forrest Brown and the collections at the Norwegian-American Historical Association at St. Olaf College offered significant insights into prevailing Norwegian-American attitudes at the turn of the century. Funding from the Washington Trust Foundation, The Delanty Fund, and a Whitworth College Faculty Research and Development Grant provided essential travel funds for two research trips to New York and Midwest states.

The surge in United States scholarship on women in the West after the first Women's West Conference in 1983 provided thought-provoking resources. I am especially indebted to Washington State University historian Susan Armitage for her generous guidance and to Gonzaga University professor Sandra Wilson for her timely comments while I was writing my doctoral dissertation on Helga's historic walk. Scholars of regional history, particularly in Washington and Minnesota, opened windows to Helga's world—most notably, Carlos Schwantes' writings on Coxey's march and early Spokane labor history, the graduate work of Nancy Engle on the Spokane suffrage movement, and Jeff Rettman on the harsher side of life in early Spokane Falls. Arlene Coulson provided exceptional research assistance gathering legal documents on Helga and Ole's life during the Spokane years, and Joan Hinkemeyer assisted with valuable resources on Colorado. Tillie Olsen's book *Silences* started my initial thinking on the silencing of family stories that surrounded all aspects of Helga's walk. I am also delighted with the innovative National History Day Association that helps teachers introduce middle-school and high-school students to the thrill of historical research; their sponsorship of the Washington State History Day Contest led to my discovery of Helga's story.

Helga's immediate extended family enthusiastically shared what little information, pictures, memories, and artifacts remain. Granddaughter Thelma Portch kept Helga's story alive with oral history and gave me the greatest glimpse of her grandmother's remarkable spirit. Helga's great-granddaughter and husband, Dorothy and Daryll Bahr, recognized the treasure they held and enriched their children's awareness of family heritage. I am thankful their son, Doug, wrote such an engaging essay for the Washington State History Day Contest, and for their daughter, Darillyn's, excellent high-school essay on her great-great-grandmother. Granddaughter Norma Lee shared important artifacts that offered another window into Helga's life, and Wanda Estby Michalek, a grand-daughter-in-law, brought memories surrounding the Mica Creek home. We are all beholden to Margaret Estby, a daughter-in-law, who secretly saved the Minnesota newspaper clippings that captured Helga and Clara's achievement and that she shared these with Thelma. Without this one act of defiance, Helga's story would have been lost forever to her extended family. Each family member added an important remnant to this story and brought pleasure to the research with their sustained interest in recovering Helga's story. They became keepers of the story and want her memory to endure, as they have discovered its power in their own heritage.

I am fortunate that editor Ivar Nelson, another per-severing Scandinavian, brought his own considerable curiosity, astute editorial questions, and thoughtful cri-tique to this manuscript—as well as bringing the skills of the professionals at the University of Idaho Press. I am grateful for the talent, commitment, and creativity of Pat Stien, a professor emeritus in theater from Whit-worth College, as we present dramatic reenactments of Helga's story to historical associations, museums, and women's groups. Her motto to "trust the story" as we dramatized the historical truth of Helga's adventure bore witness as we saw the depth of audience response to the many layers of Helga's life and to the silencing that followed her walk across America. Karlene Arguinchona, Judy Bergen, Jeri Jo Carstairs, Adam Cleaveland, Marianne Frase, Laurie Lamon, Doris Liebert, Zsuzsa Londe, Judy Palpant, Pam Parker, Annie Russell, George Scott, Monika Skerbelis, Dale Soden, and Ronald White, each offered important gifts of encouragement during the writing of this book.

My husband, Jim, a history professor, understood instinctively why this lost American story deserved to be rediscovered. As I sought to uncover the layers of mystery, he made the necessary travel a joy, read initial drafts, and asked crucial questions. Then, when family challenges caused delays, he continued to give steady and invaluable support. I will be forever thankful.